Praise for *Stand Up for Your Gifted Child*

"An outstanding resource . . . readable, well-organized, practical, and filled with excellent resources and good ideas. . . . I now know the book I will recommend to parents of gifted and talented children."

Sally Reis, Ph.D., *Professor of Educational Psychology, NEAG School of Education, University of Connecticut; President, National Association for Gifted Children*

"I applaud this much-needed manual for parent advocacy that stresses its importance, points out its benefits, and presents strategies, examples, and details of how to ensure its success. . . . A remarkable and highly valuable contribution."

Barbara Clark, Ed.D., *Professor Emeritus, California State University; President, World Council for Gifted Children*

"All children need parents to advocate for them, but advocating for gifted children is fraught with risk. Joan Smutny guides parents to intelligent, effective, and thoughtful advocacy. . . . *Stand Up for Your Gifted Child* gives parents both courage and direction for enriching their gifted children's education."

Sylvia Rimm, Ph.D., *author of* How Jane Won: 55 Successful Women Share How They Grew from Ordinary Girls to Extraordinary Women *and Clinical Professor at Case Western Reserve School of Medicine*

"Advocating for a gifted child in a typical school system may be the hardest job a parent could have. Between the myths, charges of elitism, underfunding, and negligible teacher training, parents have often had a daunting, lonely task as they sought an appropriate education for their gifted kids. *Stand Up for Your Gifted Child* changes all that. . . . Every issue I have encountered in twenty years of advocacy is covered."

Stephen Schroeder-Davis, Ph.D., *Professor of Education, University of St. Mary's Minneapolis Campus; Coordinator of Gifted Services, Elk River Area Schools; Past President, Minnesota Council for the Gifted and Talented*

"Joan Franklin Smutny is the heart and conscience of gifted education in America. . . . Immersing oneself in *Stand Up for Your Gifted Child* is comparable to having one of the nation's leading experts on gifted education as a personal consultant on call twenty-four hours a day."

Jerry Flack, Ph.D., *Professor of Education, University of Colorado; Board Member, National Association for Gifted Children*

Stand Up for Your Gifted Child

How to Make the Most of Kids' Strengths at School and at Home

JOAN FRANKLIN SMUTNY

Foreword by Jerry Flack

free spirit
PUBLiSHiNG®

Works
for kids®

Copyright © 2001 by Joan Franklin Smutny

Library of Congress Cataloging-in-Publication Data
Smutny, Joan F.
    Stand up for your gifted child : how to make the most of kids' strengths at school and at home
/ by Joan Franklin Smutny, foreword by Jerry Flack.
       p. cm.
    Includes bibliographical references (p.) and index.
    ISBN 1-57542-088-0 (pbk.)
     1. Gifted children—Education (Elementary) 2. Education, Elementary—Parent participation.
I. Title.

LC3993.22 .S48 2001
371.95'72—dc21
00-034781

At the time of this book's publication, all facts and figures cited are the most current available; all telephone numbers, addresses, and Web site URLs are accurate and active; all publications, organizations, Web sites, and other resources exist as described in this book; and all have been verified. The author and Free Spirit Publishing make no warranty or guarantee concerning the information and materials given out by organizations or content found at Web sites, and we are not responsible for any changes that occur after this book's publication. If you find an error or believe that a resource listed here is not as described, please contact Free Spirit Publishing. Parents, teachers, and other adults: We strongly urge you to monitor children's use of the Internet.

Cover design by Percolator
Interior design and illustrations by Crysten Puszczykowski

10 9 8 7 6 5 4 3 2 1
Printed in Canada

Free Spirit Publishing Inc.
217 Fifth Avenue North, Suite 200
Minneapolis, MN 55401-1299
(612) 338-2068
help4kids@freespirit.com
www.freespirit.com

The following are registered trademarks of Free Spirit Publishing Inc.:

FREE SPIRIT®
FREE SPIRIT PUBLISHING®
SELF-HELP FOR TEENS®
SELF-HELP FOR KIDS®
WORKS FOR KIDS®
THE FREE SPIRITED CLASSROOM®

free spirit
PUBLISHING®
Works for kids®

Dedication

To the thousands of parents and educators I have worked with whose vision, creativity, and perseverance in advocating for gifted children have inspired me to write this book.

Acknowledgments

This book reflects the superb assistance of the staff at Free Spirit Publishing whose editorial help and suggestions were inherent in the text's development, including Judy Galbraith, Bonnie Goldsmith, Jennifer Brannen, Darsi Dreyer, Marjorie Lisovskis, and Elizabeth Verdick. I would also like to acknowledge the work of Susan Winebrenner, Jerry Flack, Dorothy Knopper, Sandy Berger, Barbara Gosfield, and Maurice Fisher; their contributions to gifted education have inspired and advanced the cause of this book, its message, and substance.

The work of Sarah E. von Fremd during the development of this book has been invaluable. The members of the Center for Gifted at National-Louis University have been and continue to be hugely supportive—Cheryl Lind, Jenny Rinne, and Oksana and Tom Creighton.

CONTENTS

FOREWORD

by Jerry Flack, Ph.D.

Joan Franklin Smutny is the heart and conscience of gifted education in America. Her speeches, writings, workshops, and children's programs always focus on the importance of the individual gifted child or adolescent. Joan never speaks of "the gifted" in the abstract or as anonymous subjects of academic research. Young people like Natalie, Felicia, and Leth, whose stories are told in the book's pages, are the gifted children Joan celebrates. She has an immense love for these children and adolescents and is tireless and ever zealous in her advocacy for their right to an appropriately rich and stimulating education. This concern for the unique and individual gifted student makes *Stand Up for Your Gifted Child* a very special book. I cannot imagine parents reading this book without believing that the author is speaking directly and personally to them.

Immersing yourself in *Stand Up for Your Gifted Child* is comparable to having one of the nation's leading experts on gifted education as a personal consultant on call twenty-four hours a day. The book is a rich treasury of basic information about gifted children and adolescents. In it, the author provides all the essential knowledge you will need to become well-informed advocates for your children. The pages are filled with hundreds of extremely useful tips and tools. One of the greatest strengths of the book is the ease and sureness with which the author writes. Her prose is a joy to read. Her voice and vision are clear. She avoids professional jargon that might obscure the critical information parents need to know. The writing is fresh, and both understanding and understandable. You are about to have a wonderful conversation with a good listener who also gives terrific advice.

A particularly fine feature of *Stand Up for Your Gifted Child* is the use of student and parent voices. As you read the chapters of this outstanding book, you will hear the personal experiences of gifted young people and their parents. Most relate positive stories. Even those who relate negative school experiences inform us with their honesty and candor. The first-person accounts of the parents and children give the book an unusually high sense of authenticity—plus, they're just plain fun to read! The book is additionally filled with great suggestions for family outings, projects to develop creativity, ways to discover the special talents of children, and ideas for making the most of "teachable moments" at home.

Most important, *Stand Up for Your Gifted Child* is a book about advocacy. I have never read a finer or more practical book on advocacy for gifted students. First, the recommendations are eminently practical. Second, the suggestions promote collaboration between parents and the school rather than an adversarial approach. Third, all the tools and resources parents need for effective advocacy are provided.

A final thought: Although the title implies that this is a book for parents, I recommend it highly for teachers as well. The home-school equation needs to be carefully balanced. Much of the information in *Stand Up for Your Gifted Child* is vital for teachers—especially new teachers—to know. This wonderful book deserves the widest possible audience.

Stand Up for Your Gifted Child is a book not to be missed.

Jerry D. Flack, Ph.D., is Professor of Education at the University of Colorado where he is also a President's Teaching Scholar and Director of the Super Saturday Program for Gifted Children. He is a member of the Board of Directors of the National Association for Gifted Children (NAGC) and has received that organization's Early Leader and Distinguished Service awards.

INTRODUCTION

For many years, I have been listening to parents of gifted children who come to me in various states of stress or anxiety. These parents are awed and excited by the exceptional qualities they see in their children. Yet they often find their joy at being the mothers and fathers of gifted children overshadowed by a sense of responsibility, uncertainty, and isolation. They worry that they may not have the time, money, ingenuity, or stamina to give their children the support they need at home. They want their children to thrive in school, yet feel inhibited about speaking up for fear that teachers will think they are being pushy or "elitist," are overstating their children's abilities, or are asking too much for children whose intelligence and potential far exceed those of their classmates.

Maybe you share some of these concerns. I once canvassed a group of parents in one of my gifted programs to find out what challenges they faced with the schools. A father rather defensively told me that he refused to indulge in "giftedspeak" or complain about how persecuted and unhappy his daughter was when, in fact, she was managing reasonably well in the system. It's true that there are gifted children who get along well in school without special services. But why should a parent whose child is capable of excelling settle for a standard of doing "reasonably well"? It seems to me that this view misses an essential point: that all children have the right to an education that's appropriate for their particular learning needs. *Appropriate* is the key word here. When you advocate for your gifted daughter or son, you're seeking an education that fits your child's needs and abilities. This is something *every* young person deserves and is entitled to. Consider this:

Imagine you've signed up for an astronomy class that sounds tremendously interesting. For weeks, you anticipate the day when you can learn more about this subject that so intrigues you. You think about it, talk about it, plan for it excitedly. On the first day of class, you quickly discover that the course will begin with material you already know and have known for a long time. You realize with dismay that you'll be spending a month or more on this material and, after that, you'll barely scratch the surface of what you want to learn. Worse, you can't drop the class and join a more advanced one. The rule is that you have to take this class first.

This is how many gifted children in schools that don't recognize or meet their learning needs feel most of the time. Without adult intervention, these kids must endure for the whole school year the slow repetition of material they already know—or could learn lightning-fast.

I don't mean to suggest that all schools fail in the job of appropriately educating gifted children. Some schools have excellent programs in place. And it's certainly not the school's job *alone* to educate and develop children's gifts. As with any special educational needs, schools and parents must work together to achieve the best results for the child. Nevertheless, whether your child's school presently has a lot to offer or a little, your child needs your advocacy. All gifted children need advocacy. They need advocacy at home to help them recognize the depth and breadth of their abilities and discover their unique learning styles. They need advocacy at school to help them navigate their way inside and outside the classroom and acquire an appropriate education. They need advocacy at the policy level so the school, the community, and the larger society all share a vision for and a commitment to young gifted citizens.

In short, gifted kids need a parent advocate. That advocate is *you*.

WHAT IS PARENT ADVOCACY?

The dictionary defines an advocate as "one that pleads the cause of another" and "one that defends or maintains a cause." Think of your gifted child's "cause." As an observant parent, you've probably been aware of your child's unusual abilities since he* was a baby. Your love and acceptance make you particularly sensitive to these gifts and eager to support them in any way you can. You've encouraged your child by your enthusiasm, your approval, your search for resources to feed his curiosity, and your participation in all his joys and triumphs. Who, then, is better equipped than you to advocate— to plead, defend, or maintain—the cause of your gifted child's education? More to the point, who will do so if you do not?

Parent advocacy is the work you do for and on behalf of your child in order to assure that he receives an education that fits his needs and makes the most of his exceptional abilities. This advocacy doesn't require educational expertise, but rather persistence and love—qualities you already have as a parent. It calls on you to become aware of and informed about the struggles your child may experience in a world that doesn't always "see" gifted children or understand what they have to contribute. It calls on you to reach out and communicate—respectfully, assertively, and persistently— with your child's teacher and other school personnel.

---

* This book alternates the use of the pronouns "he" and "she," "her" and "him" when talking about individual gifted children. I've done this to keep the tone friendly and straightforward—it's less cumbersome than continually repeating "she or he" or "him or her." Unless specific note is made, the information applies to boys and girls alike.

It also calls on you to empower your child. Helping young people embrace their own strengths and pursue what they love most will carry them long after their school days have ended. This means that advocacy is essentially about enabling gifted kids to take charge of their own experience in a way that works best for them.

Broadly, advocacy is a frame of mind—even a way of life. It's the vision, resiliency, and unflagging determination of parents to teach their children skills for surviving and thriving. Parent advocates show their children that they can gain insight and wisdom from challenging experiences, can keep reaching for their goals even when no one seems willing or able to help, and—most important—must never give up on themselves or their abilities.

WHAT ARE YOUR RIGHTS AS A GIFTED CHILD'S PARENT?

Asking for a richer learning environment with better services is never wrong. Your child deserves to learn and progress at her own unique ability level and pace. You have the right to request this. In fact, a large part of empowering yourself as an effective advocate for your gifted child is realizing that you as a parent have specific rights:

- You have the right to know how your child's school educates its gifted population.

- You have the right to know what services exist for students whose abilities and talents require something other than, or in addition to, the standard curriculum.

- You have the right to know if your child's school is equipped to provide the kind of education she needs.

- You have the right to work with school staff to create, develop, and implement an appropriate education for your child.

- You have the right to advocate for policy-level changes in your school, district, or state.

EIGHT BENEFITS OF YOUR PARENT ADVOCACY

1. Your child will get a better education. This is a major goal of your advocacy and the most obvious benefit. In many schools, gifted children's learning needs fall at the end, not the beginning, of a long list of special educational requirements teachers must meet. Without your voice, the level of your child's education is likely to be inconsistent, mediocre—or worse. When you communicate effectively with teachers so that they understand your child's gifts and needs, when teachers know you will reliably support and monitor their efforts to appropriately educate your child, when you sustain an ongoing dialogue with your child about what's happening in school—then you're facilitating a process that's sure to improve the quality of the education your child receives. In doing this, you will gain an essential kind of power—not power *over* the school and how it teaches, but power shared *with* the school in developing a thriving program of learning for your gifted daughter or son.

2. **Your child will gain confidence and learn self-advocacy.** With your guidance, your child can begin to identify his own unique abilities, strengths, and talents and to discover the ways in which he thinks and learns best. Through your example, he can begin to recognize that he has the right to ask for the educational opportunities he needs. He can develop both the skills and the attitude that will help him assert himself and work effectively with teachers, classmates, and you—and thus become a full partner in ensuring his own education.

3. **You'll get to know your child's teacher and school, and they'll get to know you.** When you get involved in a positive way at school, everyone can benefit. The school benefits by having a caring parent willing to support it in doing its job. The teacher receives help in evaluating your child's learning needs and developing instructional approaches that can meet them. Your child has the advantage of a consistent, cohesive team approach to developing his program of learning. The ongoing dialogue that's begun will help not only in strategizing for your child's education, but also in dealing with any challenges that arise.

4. **Your efforts could mean that other children get a better education, too.** Any growth that takes place for one student in school can benefit other kids, whether they're gifted or not. Your advocacy can raise the general consciousness of a school and a teacher in regard to individual students' learning needs. This in turn can enhance the educational opportunities available for everyone.

5. **You'll get to know and work with other parents.** It's always a good idea for parents to build relationships with each other. Doing this empowers them to get involved in advancing their children's education. It helps them get to know the different students who work and learn with their own kids. As more parents get involved in their children's education, everyone's awareness and understanding is elevated. This can spill over and benefit other families and kids as well.

6. You and your child can forge a stronger relationship. As children grow, parents often become less involved in both their schooling and other aspects of their lives. While children need to develop as individuals, a parent's support and influence is still crucial. The fact that you recognize and accept your child's gifts and that you're going to be there lobbying for what she needs demonstrates your commitment to her and to her education. She knows that she can trust you to listen, hear her concerns, and work with her to resolve them. The mutual respect and understanding you develop through this experience can enrich all aspects of your life together.

7. Your family may become stronger, too. As you become sensitive to your gifted child's needs, you can't help but begin to tune in to the needs of other members of your family as well, resulting in strengthened and deepened family relationships.

8. You'll gain skills that help in your broader life. Advocacy calls on you to develop skills in listening, communicating, making judgments, asserting yourself, and negotiating. As time goes on, you'll likely find that the confidence you develop as part of this process will spill over into other areas of your life, broadening your view of the world and your capacity to impact it significantly.

HOW TO USE THIS BOOK

Stand Up for Your Gifted Child is intended to give you concrete information about giftedness and gifted education along with the tools and skills you need to become a strong advocate for your gifted child's educational needs. The book's chapters are arranged in three main parts, starting with what you can do at home to support your gifted child and moving to what you can do at school, in the community, and beyond.

The chapters begin with real-life examples parents have shared with me concerning their experiences working at home and with teachers, various school personnel, and other adults to support their gifted child. Additional parent stories are included throughout the book to illustrate and illuminate the ideas presented. You'll also find several samples of children's work. Important questions and ideas for you to consider are highlighted in text boxes punctuated with three question marks. "Find Out More" entries point you to organizations, books, Web sites, and other resources. Each chapter closes with "Take a Stand!"—a suggested action, exercise, or project that can help carry you forward on your advocacy path. Terms and "educationese" related to giftedness are explained the first time they're mentioned in the text. If you later come across a term and aren't sure what it means, check in the glossary or index at the back of the book for further information. Also at the book's end are a bibliography and an expanded list of resources for you and your child.

Much of the background information in these pages regarding policies and practices in gifted education is specific to the United States. Where possible, I've tried to point readers to information sources in Canada as well. Though there are differences in how Canadian and U.S. schools approach gifted education, a good deal of the material in this book—particularly regarding working with your child at home and with the teacher at school—is relevant and useful for Canadian readers, too.

It's my hope that you'll find this book practical, informative, and empowering. Whatever you discover within these pages, don't lose sight of your own innate capacity to support your gifted child at home and at school. No one knows your child better than you do. No one is in a better position to determine what kind of education your child needs and deserves, and to speak up and act on that behalf.

I wish you a grand adventure as you stand up for your gifted child!

Joan Franklin Smutny

Part 1
Starting at Home

Advocacy begins at home. It starts when you read the story your child has written and think, "That's a pretty sophisticated piece of writing for a third grader." Or at the supermarket when you ask yourself, "Is it unusual for a six-year-old to ask if these vegetables are genetically modified?" Or when you look at your child's first middle-school report card and wonder, "Why are his grades slipping? Were we wrong to think he was gifted?" Understanding giftedness is at the core of your ability to become an effective advocate for your gifted child. The more you know about your son's or daughter's particular gifts, the more readily you can share what you know with school staff to help meet your child's needs.

Many children display talents at home that, for one reason or another, they've never revealed at school. This can happen especially if they're not given the opportunity in school to demonstrate what they know and what interests them. Few things are more frustrating than seeing your bright, creative child do only average work in the classroom—or get perfect scores on papers and tests when you know your child isn't really learning anything new. "But," you think, "she was speaking in sentences at two. That was the year she told us she was 'dubious' about the mallards building their nest beside the road. She knew her colors and spent hours building with interlocking toy bricks."

Maybe you recognize your child's unique qualities but aren't sure that she's gifted in the way the school defines the term. Maybe you're anxious not to be thought a pushy or bragging parent. Maybe you're unsure of your ability to describe your child's exceptional strengths and so feel reluctant to talk to the school about what you've noticed at home. You want to do all you can to stand up for your gifted child. But how?

Gathering knowledge is your first step in advocating effectively for your daughter or son. What does it mean to be gifted? What are the signs and characteristics? Which characteristics does your child have? What are your child's preferred styles of thinking and learning? Unique learning differences? Strengths and weaknesses? How can you document these exceptional abilities in order to share them with school personnel? What can you do to support and nourish your child's gifts at home?

Part 1 of this book explores these questions, looking at the spectrum of ways to be gifted and the many things you can do at home to create a foundation that will enable you to advocate effectively for your gifted child.

Chapter 1
Advocacy Is . . . Understanding Giftedness

Jason's in third grade now, and, just like last year, his teacher reports that he barely says a word in class. It's such a puzzle—at home, he's so eager to join our dinnertime discussions, especially about politics. He loves to watch the news and likes to pretend he's an on-the-scene reporter. We have a drawer full of news stories he's written about our neighborhood. What on earth happens to our articulate, creative, funny kid when he sits down at his desk in school each day? Are we just imagining that he's gifted?

My daughter Laura is in fifth grade. She has a slight speech problem, which hasn't been a major issue until now. The other students have started to tease her when she answers questions. The new English teacher focuses more on her disability than on her reading and writing abilities—which are at senior-high level! Last year, Laura was pulled from the school's gifted program so she'd have time for speech therapy. I wish she could have support in *both* areas. Does having a learning difference make Laura less gifted? What does it mean to be gifted?

What does it mean to be *gifted?* The most current federal definition of what *gifted* means, as of this writing, comes from the U.S. Department of Education:

Children and youth with outstanding talent perform or show the potential for performing at remarkably high levels of accomplishment when compared with others of their age, experience, or environment.

These children and youth exhibit high performance capability in intellectual, creative, and/or artistic areas, possess an unusual leadership capacity, or excel in specific academic fields. They require services or activities not ordinarily provided by the schools.

Outstanding abilities are present in children and youth from all cultural groups, across all economic strata, and in all areas of human endeavor.*

The National Association for Gifted Children offers this definition:

There are many definitions for giftedness. They all have one element in common: A gifted person is *someone who shows, or has the potential for showing, an exceptional level of performance in one or more areas of expression.* Some of these abilities are very general and can affect a broad spectrum of the person's life, such as leadership skills or the ability to think creatively. Some are very specific talents and are only evident in particular circumstances, such as a special aptitude in mathematics, science, or music. The term *giftedness* provides a general reference to this spectrum of abilities without being specific or dependent on a single measure or index. It is generally recognized that approximately five percent of the student population, or three million children, in the United States are considered gifted.**

THREE BROAD CHARACTERISTICS OF GIFTEDNESS

It's probably no surprise to learn that giftedness is difficult to define because of its complexity. One helpful way to make sense of the thinking, learning, and behavior traits that are characteristic of gifted children is to sort them into three broad categories:

- advanced intellectual ability
- a high degree of creativity
- heightened sensibilities

Intellectual Ability

Intellectual ability includes academic aptitude—talent in areas emphasized in school, such as language arts, math, science, and social studies. More broadly, intellectual ability includes a range of skills and ways of thinking.

An academically gifted child can absorb, synthesize, and analyze information easily. He may be an advanced reader, with a precise and detailed memory. He may quickly take in new information, comprehend its meaning and application, and use logic and critical thinking in complex ways.

An academically gifted child is also curious. He asks questions constantly. He wants to know why certain things are as they are and how they got that way. He wants to understand cause-and-effect relationships.

---

* U.S. Department of Education, *National Excellence: A Case for Developing America's Talent*, Washington, DC, 1993.
** National Association for Gifted Children Web site: *www.nagc.org*, April 2001.

Parents often see advanced intellectual ability when children are quite young:

- One mother first noticed her daughter's unusual memory when, at age three, the child repeated all the stanzas of a song after hearing it only twice.

- Another parent was taken aback to hear his six-year-old son ask, "If this candy bar costs seventy-nine cents now, how much more do you think it will cost when I'm grown up?" "How do you know it will cost more?" the father asked. The boy replied, "Inflation, of course."

Academically gifted children tend to have many opinions on many subjects, read voraciously, question the logic behind certain beliefs and ideas, and enjoy discovering new facts or principles related to subjects they love.

What About Your Child?

Does your child tend to think logically? Do you find yourself surprised by the level of conversation you're having with him? Are you struck by his ability to figure out math problems in his head? Do you wonder how he came to know the things he knows? Children with exceptional intellectual ability are usually the kids most readily identified for gifted programs or instructional modifications at school—if and when the schools provide such services.

Creativity

Educators and parents have long known that creativity is a sign of giftedness. However, creative ability is difficult to measure. In a school that relies on IQ tests to identify and place gifted children (and many schools do), a child who is exceptionally imaginative or artistic won't necessarily fit the school's definition.

The mind of a creatively gifted child may go in many directions at once:

- One parent described her daughter as a girl who quickly grasped material presented in class and could easily analyze and synthesize what she learned. But the girl had problems expressing her thoughts clearly because, as she said, "I can't stop thinking at least three things at once!"

- Another parent's child tended to take little side trips from class-work into imaginative "What if?" scenarios.

Most creatively gifted kids can think logically, apply rules, find solutions, and synthesize new information. Where their creativity shows through is in the way they do all these things.

Creativity and Giftedness: Find Out More

Educator and researcher E. Paul Torrance has been a pioneer in identifying the components that underlie creative ability. One component Torrance cites is *fluency*—the fluent child is a terrific "brainstormer" who comes up with a great number of ideas in response to a problem or an assignment. Another element is *flexibility*—the child looks for alternative solutions and ideas, different or uncommon ways of doing things. *Originality* is a third characteristic—the child reviews possibilities, attempts different combinations, and sometimes discovers or invents something new. A fourth creative quality is *elaboration*—the child is good at analyzing and fine-tuning ideas, applying discoveries and creations to new situations. Check out this book to learn more about Torrance's research on the creative process:

Making the Creative Leap Beyond . . . by E. Paul Torrance and H. Tammy Safter (Buffalo, NY: CEF Press, 1999). The authors explore the processes of creativity and the motivations that drive creative people to search, explore, experiment, and innovate. The book shows how creative people sense problems—gaps in knowledge or something askew in a situation—and how this impels them to formulate hypotheses and arrive at a new thought or concept.

Creative kids tend to push logic to its limits. Instead of saying, "If this is so, then this must also be so," they will say, "If this rule applies here, can it also apply to this other situation? Can I adjust it to make it work? If not, why not?" They look for what's new, different, unfamiliar. They'll spend time (maybe too much time) looking for alternative approaches to assignments they find dull. Their school papers may be framed in clever little doodles. Some creative kids are daydreamers; staying on the beaten path is hard for them. They always want to know what's around the corner, up that next hill, beyond the horizon.

You'll notice that this view of creativity doesn't mention having a single specific talent. A child who has a particular musical or artistic talent may or may not be gifted in the broad sense of the word. A talented child who is creatively gifted is likely to have several talents, to be passionate in pursuing them, and to be a creative thinker as well.

Creatively gifted children sometimes face a difficult situation, both in and out of school. The world around them seems more interested in answers, solutions, and concrete information than in questions, processes, and enigmas. For some kids, creativity is so tied to their identity that they often feel part of another universe.

I have spoken with many parents about creativity in gifted young people, particularly as it applies to testing. Creatively gifted kids often feel stress and frustration when they take tests asking for one right answer to a question or problem. Many fall back on guessing just to get through the experience. Others run out of time and leave many items unanswered. When I've talked to these students about their experiences, many of them say, in effect, "I couldn't decide on an answer because it all depends on how you look at it."

What About Your Child?

What does your child most love to do? Does she invent or modify objects to use in unusual ways? Improvise with toys or games? Have a vivid imagination? Is she happiest when she's free to follow her own thoughts and form her own conclusions? To some extent, creative children need advocacy the most. They have a tendency to believe something's wrong with them because they think so differently from other kids.

Heightened Sensibilities

Sensibility is a child's capacity to be involved with something in a deep, internal way. Gifted kids are often extremely sensitive, tending to absorb the world through every pore. Life provides them with multiple and complex sensations. These kids may be stopped cold by the sight of Canadian geese flying south at dusk, overwhelmed by the pounding beat from a passing car radio, energized by blowing leaves, fascinated by a thunderstorm. They're often unusually conscious of appeals to their senses—the feel of mud squishing through their toes, the spicy smell of baking gingerbread, the warmth of a fire near cold feet.

Yesterday, my six-year-old son and I were reading a book that involved baking bread. In the middle of the story, he suddenly turned to me and said, "Daddy, why don't we make our own bread? I know the ingredients we need and I just think the feeling of kneading dough would be so wonderful." Then he talked about the smell of baking bread and how nice it is to spread butter on warm bread and watch it melt. I get about five observations like this a day. I am so lucky!

Most children respond to sights, sounds, smells, and sensations, but gifted kids tend to feel everything in more depth and detail. Their impressions often stay with them a long time.

Kids may also express their giftedness through unusually empathic responses to people. They may be deeply attuned to the circumstances and feelings of family members, friends, and classmates. Sometimes they become sad when they feel powerless to help someone. Gifted kids might offer friendship to an ostracized classmate, be especially thoughtful toward an unhappy family member, or cry about the mistreatment of an animal. They may ask questions and express concern about world problems—poverty, war, pollution.

Fall's Taste

If fall had a taste it would taste
Golden as the fallen leaves
Warm and satisfying as soup
Yet sometimes strong and fierce as the wind
Solid as the frozen lakes
Crisp and cool as fresh leaves
Adventurous as migrating geese
Cozy and comfortable as fire
Quacky and excited like the ducks
If fall had a taste at all.

—Martha, grade 4

A mournful sky
Shivering
Casting waves of unhappiness through her veins
Thoughtful limbs
Reach upward to plant a kiss on a frowning thought
comforting
A seed
Soon to change the color of Mother sky to a rich healthy sapphire blue
that will burn away her black cape of troubles
Melt them down to tiny drops
Letting them fall away to cool the Earth
Then thank her fellow trees
And invite them up her stairway for tea, as an honor for their kindness

—Kendall, grade 5

Another sensitivity commonly found among gifted kids is intuition—exceptional insight that enables a child to see and feel things well beyond his years, to "read" a person or situation. An intuitive child probes beyond surface meanings and tries to interpret what he hears and sees in different ways. Intuition may appear while a child works out a new way to do a math problem. He may say, "I don't know how I figured this out, but I just had a hunch it might work." Parents may discover a child's intuition when he's able to predict—before anyone else in the family—what's likely to happen next in a TV show.

Intuition sometimes seems to bring a child insights without involving any rational process. An intuitive child will suddenly sense something he can't quite explain logically. He may have picked up a subtle clue (from body language or tone of voice). He may simply have a strong hunch he's on the right track.

When Sam was six, we took in relatives who'd lost their jobs and had to sell their home. They stayed with us for six months, got back on their feet, and bought a new home. A few days after they left, Sam told me, "It'll be nice for them to have a new house. They were so sad when they were living here." This was true—but we'd had no idea Sam was picking up on their feelings. No one told him they were sad, and our relatives had taken care to be upbeat.

For many gifted children, yet another part of emotional sensitivity is perfectionism. From an early age, gifted children become accustomed to being praised for the amazing things they say and do. Soon, their ability and achievements may become tied to pleasing their parents, teachers, and peers. They often begin to expect themselves to excel at everything they do. It's not unusual for gifted children to feel that nothing they do is ever "good enough." A drive for excellence can easily evolve into a "need" to be perfect: to be the best, know the most, and achieve the highest. Perfectionistic children may find it hard to accept criticism, yet be extremely critical of themselves and others. They might put off starting projects they feel they can't do perfectly. They may feel sad, frightened, or stressed some or much of the time. They may worry so much about the future that they can't embrace the moment.

Emotional Giftedness: Find Out More

Daniel Goleman has written books about "emotional intelligence." He describes qualities that add up to "a different way of being smart": self-awareness, impulse control, persistence, zeal, self-motivation, empathy, and social skills. People with emotional intelligence understand and manage their feelings, make good decisions, and are exceptionally good at cooperation, negotiation, leadership, and teamwork. They tend to form deep, lasting relationships. Goleman argues convincingly that *how* we use our intelligence is more important than how much intelligence we have. To read more, check out this book:

Emotional Intelligence: Why It Can Matter More than IQ by Daniel Goleman (New York: Bantam Books, 1997). Goleman effectively argues that the emotions relate to cognition and cognitive functioning. He points out ways in which the ability to control one's impulses and persist in an effort influences decision making and achievement. He shows how a gifted child's awareness of and sensitivity to feelings enables that child to negotiate, take on leadership roles, and resolve social or emotional problems.

What About Your Child?

Does your child respond in an intensely deep or detailed way to what he sees, hears, touches, tastes, and smells? Is he unusually attuned to other people's feelings? Does he feel deeply about many things? Is he able to "read" people and situations? Many gifted children are extremely intense, unusually aware of their own moods and emotions, and capable of thinking and feeling deeply about many things.

BRIGHT VS. GIFTED: WHAT'S THE DIFFERENCE?

In reading about these characteristics, you probably see a variety of different aspects that describe your child. Possibly you're still confused about whether your child is gifted. Is there a difference between being bright and being gifted? Yes. In her book *You Know Your Child Is Gifted When . . .* , Judy Galbraith makes the point that gifted kids are "often so much *more* of everything than other kids their age—more intense, curious, challenging, frustrating, sensitive, passionate. They *know* so much more. They *learn* so much faster. They *feel* so deeply." Galbraith offers this example:

> Think about what it means to read at age 4. . . . Not only do you have a skill that most other kids your age don't have, but reading changes your life forever. You have access to information and ideas, stories and fictional characters. Your world broadens beyond your family, school, and community. You're exposed to the thoughts, feelings, and imaginations of adult writers from other times and places. As a result, your thinking skills race ahead of other children your age. Reading isn't just a skill, like tying your shoes. It's a profound awakening.*

There *is* a difference between being bright and being gifted. Often that difference has to do with the *degree* of a child's ability or talent. The following chart compares some of the differences. In looking at the chart, keep in mind that no two gifted children are alike and that few, if any, children will be gifted in all of the ways depicted on the chart:

---

* *You Know Your Child Is Gifted When . . . A Beginner's Guide to Life on the Bright Side* by Judy Galbraith, M.A., Minneapolis: Free Spirit Publishing, 2000, page 20. Used by permission.

The bright child	The gifted child
Knows the answers.	Asks the questions.
Is interested.	Is extremely curious.
Pays attention.	Gets involved physically and mentally.
Works hard.	Plays around, still gets good grades/test scores.
Answers questions.	Questions the answers.
Enjoys same-age peers.	Prefers adults or older children.
Learns easily.	Is bored. Already knew the answers.
Listens well.	Shows strong feelings and opinions.
Readily takes in information.	Processes information and applies it more broadly, with greater complexity, or in unique ways.
Seeks clear, fast solutions.	Explores problems in depth.
Has a unique talent.	Has many talents.
Likes to finish a project.	Enjoys the process more than the end product.
Is self-satisfied.	Is highly critical of self (perfectionistic).
Is insightful.	Is extraordinarily intuitive.**

OTHER DIMENSIONS OF GIFTEDNESS

Giftedness reveals itself in many ways. While schools often identify young people with high academic ability, they're less likely to identify gifted children who learn in unique ways, who are creatively gifted, or whose exceptional abilities are expressed through sensitivities rather than performance on tests.

It's helpful to know, too, that while some gifted kids excel in school, some do not. For one thing, most kids aren't gifted at everything and most develop at different rates. Gifted children's intellectual development is usually ahead of their physical and emotional development. A gifted child may talk like an adult but have temper tantrums like the child he is. He may think of projects he'd like to do but lack the motor skills to do them. This is called *asynchronous development,* and it can be frustrating and confusing for both parents and kids.

** Adapted from "The Gifted and Talented Child," written by Janet Szabos Robbins, Maryland Council for Gifted & Talented, Inc., PO Box 12221, Silver Spring, MD 20908. Used by permission.

A while ago I spoke with a parent who was puzzled about her young daughter's ability. She believed the girl couldn't be gifted because she wasn't reading or writing above her grade level, yet she'd recently surprised her mother with a series of dinosaurs she'd drawn and meticulously labeled. This parent was surprised to learn that, in some children, giftedness doesn't show itself in advanced reading and writing skills. It can take time for these skills to catch up with a child's exceptional intellect.

A variety of circumstances or conditions can influence the way gifted children behave, the interests they pursue, and how teachers—and sometimes parents—perceive them:

Gifted children with disabilities. A physical, emotional, or learning disability may overshadow a gifted child's abilities and talents. It's not unusual for a child to be "twice exceptional"—to be gifted and also have a disability. When this is the case, schools often tend to focus on the disability rather than the whole child, leaving the young person's exceptional abilities unnoticed and underchallenged.

Timing of identification at school. In an ideal world, schools would identify gifted kids at least as early as kindergarten. Most schools don't do this, however, because evaluating giftedness in children who can't yet take paper-and-pencil tests requires more staff resources than many schools have. Thus, schools often assess giftedness at the end of second grade or the beginning of third grade (or later). As a result, gifted kindergarten and primary-age children may not be challenged to reach their potential in the classroom. This early experience with school can leave children bored and frustrated and could impede their learning later on. Today, educators' interest in identifying giftedness earlier is growing, but addressing the needs of young gifted children still has a long way to go.

Gifted girls. As they move into upper-elementary and middle school, girls often confront social pressures and biases that may cause them to suppress their talents and underachieve. As early as third grade, many girls tend to become sensitive about what their classmates think of them. Often they're teased about being different or laughed at because of their intellectual curiosity. They may begin to believe that they aren't as intelligent or don't know as much as people think they do. This "imposter's syndrome" can lead some gifted girls to censor themselves and camouflage their abilities at school. Their joy in their gifts is clouded by the realization that other kids their age find them "weird" or "geeky."

Gifted girls often face gender stereotyping from the education system and their teachers as well as their peers. Classroom behaviors that, in boys, are considered acceptable signs of enthusiastic learning may be ignored or even frowned on in girls. Uncomfortable with competition, some gifted girls retreat into mediocrity. They often are not provided with the array of opportunities, including group work and independent study, that would draw them out of intellectual hiding.

Gifted boys. Boys gifted in areas other than math and science may face similar pressures to conform—particularly boys who aren't athletic. Some boys may put their gifts "under cover" to avoid being teased; others may continue to pursue their interests and abilities but feel the pain of being outsiders.

Boys in primary and elementary school who have a lot of energy find it difficult to sit still and work quietly. Some are diagnosed, rightly or wrongly, as having ADHD (attention deficit hyperactivity disorder). With many high-energy gifted boys, this means the focus moves away from their giftedness and toward dealing with behavior issues.

Middle and high school. Often gifted kids whose experiences in the lower grades challenged and stimulated them are stopped short when they arrive at middle school or high school. In the upper grades there may be few programs or systems in place for meeting the needs of gifted students. The close teacher-child relationships of elementary school aren't possible in this new setting, and the scheduling of classes in 50-minute blocks makes it less convenient for teachers to adapt the curriculum. In classes, students are often grouped *heterogeneously*—not by ability—most or all of the time. Intellectually gifted kids don't always thrive in this setting, unless the school's program allows for flexibility in grouping and regrouping students into small groups of children with varying strengths and abilities.

It's not unusual for a gifted child to breeze through elementary school without developing the study skills or stick-to-itiveness they'll need to handle a more diversified curriculum in middle school. A child may wonder, "Why is this so hard? Have I lost IQ points?" The result can be that the child ceases to excel or covers up this uncertainty by troublemaking or clowning around.

Cultural factors. Gifted kids from minority or out-of-the-mainstream groups face a variety of obstacles that complicate a parent's search for an appropriate education for a child. For example, in an environment where gifted children are singled out, a high-ability child from a family whose culture is group-oriented may not be as readily identified and may not be comfortable as the focus of a teacher's attention. A child who's recently arrived from another country may not be proficient in English, and thus may have her true abilities masked by difficulties with reading and writing in English.

Family stresses. Economic, work, and family pressures can leave a parent little time or energy to communicate with teachers and advocate for an appropriate education for a gifted child. Though it's extremely useful for a teacher to know when a child's family is dealing with difficulties, parents often don't choose to share this information with anyone at the school. The result can be that a gifted child who's preoccupied with worries about home doesn't perform up to her ability, begins to have behavior problems that overshadow or change the quality of her schoolwork, or is marginalized because the teacher doesn't sense that the parent is interested in working with the school in the interest of the child.

Yes, gifted kids and their families face many challenges! That's why your advocacy is so important. Chapter 1 has given you a broad look at what it means to be gifted—a context from and through which to think about the needs and circumstances of gifted children. The next step is to understand your child's particular gifts. Knowing your child's strengths, weaknesses, and personal circumstances gives you a baseline for exploring different learning options and resources at school.

Take a Stand!

On pages 21–23 you'll find a reproducible form called "Checklist of My Child's Traits." Take some time now to sit down in a quiet place, think about your child, and complete the checklist, checking those items that are *usually* or *often* true of your child. In the space provided at the end of the checklist, note any traits and characteristics not included on the checklist as well as other factors (such as a disability, hyperactivity, or cultural considerations) you feel are important in understanding your child's giftedness. Then go on to Chapter 2 to explore ways to interpret and document what you know and are learning about your gifted child.

CHECKLIST OF MY CHILD'S TRAITS

Check any items that *usually* or *often* apply to your child.

_____ 1. Enjoys or prefers to work and play independently.

_____ 2. Can "multitask"—concentrate on two or three activities at once.

_____ 3. Prefers the company of older kids and adults to that of children his/her own age.

_____ 4. Loves to read or look through books.

_____ 5. Reads books and magazines geared for older kids and adults.

_____ 6. Shows interest in cause-and-effect relationships.

_____ 7. Learns quickly and applies knowledge easily.

_____ 8. Shows an unusual grasp of logic.

_____ 9. Has an advanced vocabulary for his/her age.

_____ 10. Seems extremely precocious—talks or thinks like an adult.

_____ 11. Enjoys making discoveries on his/her own and solving problems in his/her own way.

_____ 12. Likes to play with words.

_____ 13. Resists conforming, playing games, or doing projects with other kids the same age.

_____ 14. Shows asynchronous (uneven) development—may be highly precocious cognitively, while demonstrating age-appropriate or even delayed development emotionally or socially. (*Example:* An 8-year-old who understands and can avidly explain the role of chlorophyll in the process of photosynthesis, but struggles with reading all the words in a picture book.)

_____ 15. Loves math games, playing with number concepts, and figuring out how to solve math problems in unique ways.

more ▶▶

Checklist of My Child's Traits (continued)

_____ 16. Wants to know the reasons for rules—and the reasons behind the reasons.

_____ 17. Discusses or elaborates on ideas in complex, unusual ways.

_____ 18. Sees many possible answers to questions or solutions to problems.

_____ 19. Loves to know and give reasons for everything.

_____ 20. Is extremely curious, asks lots of questions, and questions the answers.

_____ 21. Shows leadership in organizing games and activities and in resolving disputes.

_____ 22. Has a long attention span for things that interest him/her.

_____ 23. Becomes so involved that he/she is not aware of anything else.

_____ 24. Has many unusual hobbies or interests.

_____ 25. Has elaborate collections and is passionate about them.

_____ 26. Has a vivid imagination.

_____ 27. Invents games, toys, and other devices.

_____ 28. Thinks of new ways to do things.

_____ 29. Likes to create by drawing, painting, writing, building, experimenting, storytelling, or inventing.

_____ 30. Enjoys singing, playing an instrument, dancing or moving rhythmically, or pantomime.

_____ 31. Responds to music, is able to improvise tunes and rhythms, or composes songs.

_____ 32. Sees patterns and connections that others don't see, even among things that are apparently unrelated.

more ▶▶

Checklist of My Child's Traits (continued)

_____ 33. Argues or debates about the logic of ideas, rules, or actions.

_____ 34. Tends to rebel against what's routine or predictable.

_____ 35. Has a well-developed sense of humor.

_____ 36. Absorbs the speech patterns and vocabulary of different people and imitates them in stories, music, skits, comedy routines, or games.

_____ 37. Is very active; has trouble sitting still.

_____ 38. Likes to discuss abstract ideas like God, love, justice, and equality.

_____ 39. Expresses unusual sensitivity to what is seen, heard, touched, tasted, and smelled.

_____ 40. Shows sensitivity to the feelings of others and empathy in response to other people's troubles.

_____ 41. Expresses concern about world problems such as endangered animals, racism, pollution, and poverty.

_____ 42. Shows a willingness to follow intuitive hunches even if they can't immediately be justified.

_____ 43. Demonstrates high energy, focus, and intensity.

_____ 44. Is frustrated by imperfection in others and in himself/herself.

_____ 45. Is extra sensitive to criticism.

_____ 46. Shows intuitive sensitivity to spiritual values and beliefs; ponders philosophical issues.

Describe other characteristics that _usually_ or _often_ apply to your child, as well as other factors you feel are important in understanding your child's giftedness. If you need more space, use the back of your photocopied page.

_____

_____

Chapter 2
Advocacy Is . . . Understanding Your Child's Gifts

Our son Jared is curious about how everything and anything works. We've always believed he has exceptional abilities, so we couldn't understand why he was slow to learn to read and why he never seemed to enjoy reading. The only things he liked to read were instruction manuals and other how-to books. When Jared was ten, we took a car trip and asked him to be the navigator. He loved reading the maps, checking the compass, and figuring out alternate routes and side trips. Jared's also a whiz at assembling things—he can work with the most complex, hard-to-follow directions and diagrams. We've realized that Jared simply doesn't like to just sit down and read. He wants to do things, make things, experiment, and figure things out. Sure, we hope he'll learn to love reading for its own sake some day. But at this point, we've stopped worrying about it.

Last night my first grader, Rena, insisted we couldn't put a certain two storybooks side by side on the shelf. "You can't put them next to each other, Mom!" she told me. "The people in one may fall into the other story!" She went on to explain what she thinks happens "when stories bump into each other." "Some of them might not get along in the same world." Rena's imagination has always been amazing.

It's one thing to know in your heart that you have a gifted child. It's another thing to identify the *ways* in which your child is gifted and *how* your son or daughter shows those gifts.

START WITH YOUR CHECKLIST

The checklist in Chapter 1 (pages 21–23) provides a starting point for deepening your understanding of your child's giftedness. If you haven't already completed the checklist, do so now. When you're done, consider what the checklist has to tell you. Start by grouping your observations.

Group Your Child's Broad Areas of Giftedness

First, consider whether and how your child is gifted in each of the three broad categories discussed in Chapter 1: intellectual abilities, creativity, and heightened sensibilities. The items on the checklist are loosely arranged into these three categories, though many of the characteristics overlap to some degree. On the checklist:

- Items 1–22 reflect many of the ways in which children demonstrate exceptional intellectual or academic abilities.

- Items 13–36 generally highlight the signs of a creatively gifted child.

- Items 36–46 depict heightened sensibilities, emotions, and sensitivities.

If you listed other characteristics, consider the traits you've noted in terms of intelligence, creativity, and sensibility. The checklist may show that your child's strengths lie in one or even two of the categories, but probably not all three. While most kids will have a few traits from each category, it's rare for a child to be gifted intellectually, creatively, *and* in terms of sensibilities.

Next, take a look at the information from the checklist through another lens: how your child learns.

IDENTIFY HOW YOUR CHILD LEARNS BEST

Over the past twenty years, the way we understand human intelligence has significantly changed. People used to assume that intelligence was uniform, measurable, and unchanging, that it could be quantified into an "intelligence quotient," or IQ. Scores on IQ tests have for a long time largely determined how children are placed and taught in school, as well as what opportunities are made available to them. To a great extent, this situation persists in U.S. schools.

Still, in recent years, many educators, researchers, and parents have questioned the reliability of tests to measure such a complicated phenomenon as human intelligence. Do tests primarily assess actual intelligence, or a child's test-taking skills? This question has become more important as new theories about how gifted children learn begin to challenge long-held assumptions.

New Definitions of Learning and Intelligence

In Chapter 1 you read about the theories of E. Paul Torrance and Daniel Goleman in regard to creative and emotional aspects of giftedness. The work of two other researchers has deepened and broadened our understanding of how children—especially gifted children—think and learn.

Sternberg's Theory: Three Dimensions of Intelligence

Researcher Robert Sternberg developed a model of how the mind processes information. His model describes giftedness in terms of the ability to do three distinct things: analyze, synthesize, and apply thinking to practical problems. Gifted children, he claims, can integrate these three abilities and use each one in a way that will best solve a problem or generate a new idea. Sternberg's theory is important, because it places in question the validity of IQ tests as a primary measure of giftedness. While IQ tests *can* measure a child's ability to analyze, they won't necessarily identify creative children who can produce novel ideas or who can approach problems from new perspectives. And for Sternberg, the ability to solve problems, to know what to do in real-life situations, is an important part of intelligence. The items on the checklist that correlate to Sternberg's model include 1, 6, 7, 8, 11, 15, 18, 20, and 28.

Gardner's Theory: Multiple Intelligences

The research of Howard Gardner has expanded the meaning of intelligence even further. Gardner believes that there are at least eight "intelligences"— eight different ways of taking in information and thinking about it—and that each individual has relative strengths and weaknesses among these intelligences. Gardner's theory of "multiple intelligences" applies to all children, but it has enabled gifted educators to explore and understand the unique ability profile of individual gifted students. It can be helpful in discovering how children absorb and use information. As you'll see, Gardner's use of the word *intelligence* embraces thinking that is intellectual, creative, and "sense-related."

Linguistic intelligence. The linguistically intelligent child learns best by reading, speaking, telling, discussing, paying attention to word sounds and meanings, memorizing, building vocabulary, and telling stories. Linguistic intelligence is reflected on the checklist in items 4, 5, 9, and 12.

Logical-mathematical intelligence. A child whose preferred intelligence is logical-mathematical enjoys and excels at solving problems. This child perceives patterns, unearths underlying processes, makes calculations easily, grasps number and symbol concepts, and likes games and brainteasers that require logic and abstract reasoning. On the checklist, items 8, 11, 16, and 18 relate to logical-mathematical intelligence.

Visual-spatial intelligence. A child with strong visual-spatial intelligence understands how objects and figures relate in three-dimensional space, can rotate shapes mentally and "see" them from all angles, can create representations and then transfer them to other situations, and enjoys chess, puzzles, maps, drawing, designing, and building. If this is one of your child's preferred intelligences, you probably checked many of items 15, 17, 18, 25, 28, 29, and 32.

Bodily-kinesthetic intelligence. A young person with bodily-kinesthetic intelligence has excellent body and/or fine motor control, moves easily and gracefully, is good at handling and manipulating objects, and generally prefers to learn by doing. This child may enjoy a range of activities from gymnastics, dance, and sports to crafts, carpentry, hands-on science, and dramatic arts. The items on the checklist that correspond to this intelligence are 1, 30, 36, 37, 39, and 43.

Musical intelligence. Musical children are sensitive to rhythm, melody, musical patterns, tempo, pitch, and harmony. They can easily reproduce melodies heard only once, can "hear" different parts of a musical piece simultaneously, hum and sing a lot, and may improvise with rhythms or melodies. Items 30, 31, 36, and 39 on the checklist point to musical intelligence.

Interpersonal intelligence. Interpersonal intelligence means that the child gets along well with others, has great empathy for other people, is intuitive, and is a good organizer, leader, mediator, and communicator. Traits from the checklist that demonstrate interpersonal intelligence are 3, 10, 18, 21, 32, 33, 40, 42, and 43.

Intrapersonal intelligence. The child with this preferred intelligence has keen personal insight, understands his own strengths and feelings, likes to work independently, is good at managing emotions and goals, and may use music, dance, journals, or crafts as creative forms of self-expression. Several items on the checklist are part of interpersonal intelligence, including 1, 11, 14, 23, 25, 29, 34, 35, 39, 42, 44, 45, and 46.

Naturalist intelligence. Young naturalists are keen observers of various plants and animals, demonstrate an advanced understanding of ecology and the different elements of the natural world, and love to sort, classify, and order just about anything. Items on the checklist that show naturalist intelligence include 5, 7, 11, 20, 25, 32, 39, 41, and 43.

Intelligence and Giftedness: Find Out **More**

Here are three readings that will give you more insight into intelligence and giftedness:

Eight Ways of Knowing: Teaching for Multiple Intelligences, 3rd ed. by David Lazear (Palatine, IL: Skylight Publishing, 1998). Lazear does a good job of explaining how to apply Gardner's theory to learning styles and puts multiple intelligences into real situations. A handbook of techniques, it shows how to translate these intelligences into learning activities that can develop children's cognitive abilities. An excellent resource for parents and teachers looking for a practical, down-to-earth guide to multiple intelligences.

"Emotional Giftedness: The Measure of Intrapersonal Intelligence" by Michael Piechowski, in *Handbook of Gifted Education*, edited by Nicholas Colangelo and Gary A. Davis, 2nd ed. (Needham Heights, MA: Allyn & Bacon, 1997), pages 366–381. In this chapter, Piechowski extends Gardner's concept of intrapersonal intelligence (knowledge of self) and gives it a deeper, more detailed treatment. He combines the ideas of emotional giftedness, emotional growth, and moral sensitivity with a focus on self-evaluation and inner transformation. He argues that intrapersonal intelligence is not just part of how people function but is, in the deepest sense, the development of a person as a whole being.

Intelligence Reframed: Multiple Intelligences for the 21st Century by Howard Gardner (New York: Basic Books, 2000). Gardner reviews intelligence theory, reintroduces and describes his concept of multiple intelligences, and considers other intelligences that may exist beyond those he's identified (such as moral intelligence). He also looks at how multiple intelligences apply to children's learning in school.

Our understanding of what intelligence is continues to evolve. Today, many schools recognize that children have different learning and thinking styles, and many teachers agree that IQ isn't the only measure of giftedness. But in most cases, assessment of children for gifted programming has not caught up with what research is telling us about the complexity of intelligence. Your observation at home of how your child learns best—of his "preferred intelligences"—is powerful information you can bring to the table when working with the school to identify and develop your child's gifts. It can expand the view of your child and can increase a teacher's ability to teach, work with, and understand him. You can also use this information to help you focus and expand the activities and opportunities your child pursues at home.

CONSIDER OTHER THINGS YOU KNOW ABOUT YOUR CHILD

You know your child better than anyone—no one has a more complete picture of the mix of qualities that make her the unique child she is. In considering what your gifted child needs in order to thrive at home and at school, it's important to identify the full range of facets that push and pull her as she develops, learns, and grows.

As a parent advocate, you will need to work closely with the school so that your child's potential is fully realized. Before you can communicate clearly with the teacher, you need to clarify in your own mind all the elements that affect your child's learning.

Natalie once loved science more than anything and took first place at the science fair in fifth grade. When she started middle school, she couldn't wait to join the science club, but she soon found she was the only girl attending the after-school meetings. Recently Natalie told her dad she wants to quit the club. "I want to hang out with Lily and Anne," she explained. "I'll be left out of everything if I stay in the science club." Natalie's dad is worried about his daughter. He hates to see her lose interest in the subject she's always enjoyed the most.

Eight-year-old Andreas has a speech impediment and leaves the classroom for speech therapy three times a week. Away from school, he's studying amphibian behavior by watching interactive videos, doing research on the Internet, and volunteering at the zoo with his mom. His science and reading grades are barely average. Andreas's mom knows her son should be performing better in class, but she doesn't want to question what the school is doing. After all, the family's lucky that Andreas can get help with his speech difficulties. She reminds Andreas of this often, especially when he complains that he doesn't want to go to school.

Both Natalie and Andreas are gifted children. At school, both are experiencing things that are diverting and masking their abilities. Their parents know—probably better than their teachers—that their children's tremendous potential is being blocked by factors that don't show up on intelligence tests, or even in what teachers observe in school. Both of these children need their parents' advocacy. Both need their parents to listen, offer guidance, strengthen their family relationship, and find a way to communicate with school about all of the qualities and experiences that shape these two gifted children.

As with this father and mother, your role as an advocate calls on you to look at the whole picture, a picture that can change as your child grows. The checklist you've completed can serve as a beginning record for charting that picture.

KEEP TRACK OF WHAT YOU SEE

I've often heard parents say, "I really should write down the things my daughter says" or "My son is always amazing us with his projects. I know I should keep a record of them all, but I never get around to it." The fact is, writing your observations and keeping samples of your child's work on a regular basis can be both an ongoing record of your child's giftedness for you and your family *and* a valuable tool for effective advocacy. When you talk with a teacher or administrator about your child, it's important to have a clear record of what you've observed at home.

Use a Notebook

If you don't already have a notebook or journal where you record observations about your child, start one today. The kind of notebook you use will depend on your personal style: You'll want to choose something that will allow you to add to it easily and often. If you're inclined to write a good deal, you might consider a thick, college-ruled notebook. Tape an envelope inside the notebook's cover for storing notes and scraps of paper, or buy a notebook that has pocketed dividers. It's not necessary to take lengthy notes or keep a detailed diary, though, and another option is to use a folder with pockets and metal tabs that will secure three-hole-punched sheets of paper.

You may want to carry the notebook with you and write in it regularly, or you might jot notes on slips of paper—a sentence or two to remind you of something your child said or did—and transfer the notes to your notebook periodically. The very process of writing about your child can provide insights that will be useful guides for talking with teachers and for helping you support your child's talents more effectively. Talk with other adults, too—when you share stories about things your child said or did, you keep these memories alive and sharpen your perceptions. Make notes about these conversations as well. And get in the habit of dating each entry. Writing over a period of time, you may begin to notice patterns—recurring behaviors, interests, and abilities—that show how your child demonstrates his gifts.

If you prefer to write on a computer, choose a notebook or folder that will let you store printouts. Some people find it easier to dictate their thoughts and observations into a tape recorder. You can do this, too, and take time occasionally to listen to your remarks and write brief notes or summaries of your comments.

As soon as you start your notebook, date your completed checklist and tape or store it inside. Also place in the notebook test results and report cards that show a record of your child's performance in school. From time to time, photocopy the checklist from this book and complete it again. It can be fascinating to see how your child develops, which—if any—characteristics seem to change, and what other factors exert their influence on your gifted child.

4/23
Erik working on new map-distribution of gorillas in central Africa! Has contact researcher at U.

4/27
E finished sketching major forests of Congo. Is now working on Uganda and Rwanda.

4/30
E is updating files from new info he's found on Net. Wants to design Web site for kids to learn about gorillas, how to help them.

Nov. 13—Molly amazed me today when she said she wants to be an archeologist. She saw a show on the Discovery Channel about people digging for the remains of an old city in Morocco. "I just think it would be interesting to find things from people who lived on earth thousands of years ago." She showed me some books from the school library and said she'd better start training now because "you know, Mom, there's no classes in archeology at school."

Nov. 18—Molly said, out of the blue: "Do you think there'll be a day in the future when our city will be dug out by some archeologists?"

Put Together a Portfolio

When your child does exceptional work, save it. Store art and science projects, stories, inventions, and other things in a big box or a cupboard. Also include photographs or videotapes of projects, performances, and special events. Go through this "portfolio" with your child once in a while. This shared time can be a great way to support and encourage your child, especially if he's feeling unsure of himself, despondent, or concerned about his school performance.

As an advocate, your collection is also a treasure trove when you want to show the school evidence of your child's talents. I've met children whose intellectual or creative lives begin only when they get home. They don't distinguish themselves in any way in the classroom, and teachers consider them average students. At home, however, these children may invent, read advanced books, or work on complex projects. If you recognize your child in this description, you'd do well to collect samples of his work. As with your notebook, the items in this portfolio can be telling ways of demonstrating what your child can do and what kinds of educational opportunities he needs.

In Chapter 8, pages 103–108, you'll find suggestions for effectively sharing information from the notebook and portfolio with school personnel.

Get started with a system for keeping track of your observations about your gifted child. Buy and set up your notebook and, together with your child, organize a portfolio. This activity can serve as a warm-up for reading Chapter 3, where you'll look more closely at ways to foster your relationship with your child at home.

Chapter 3
Advocacy Is . . .
Helping Your Child Cope with
Friendships, Family, and Feelings

My daughter Mandy is in third grade, and she still has no friends her own age. She comes home after school and plays with the kids next door, a girl three years older and the girl's younger brother, a year younger than Mandy. She doesn't have all that much in common with either of them, and I know she's lonely.

Our sixth-grade son Thuong is having a hard year. We're not sure exactly what's going on because he won't talk to us about it. He's still doing very well in school, as always. But he's moody and seems unhappy. I know this is how many kids start adolescence, but Thuong used to have so many interests! Now he just shuts himself up in the bedroom with the music blaring, stares at the ceiling, or spends hours on the Internet. We want him to know that we care and want to help, but he seems anti-parent right now. How can we get him to open up to us?

There's so much emphasis today on what parents should do for their children. Yet what matters more than doing "all the right things" is your own strong relationship with your child. It's not so much what you *do* for your child, but what you *are* to him that counts. A strong relationship means that your child knows your love is unconditional, a constant in his life. It means you and your child are open with each other, able to disagree and still respect differences of opinion, comfortable with a free exchange of ideas. A supportive family environment helps keep your gifted child afloat, even if he's unhappy or underchallenged in school.

In my work with parents of gifted children, certain questions come up again and again:

- What can I do to help my child make friends and feel less alone?

- How can I help my child cope with being teased?

- What are strategies for helping a highly sensitive child deal with intense excitement, anxiety, fears, failure, and disappointment?

- How can I help my child learn to accept mistakes as part of learning? What is the line between encouraging my child to succeed and burdening him with my high expectations?

As a parent, you can't wave a magic wand and make these and other challenges faced by your gifted child disappear. What you can do is consider thoughtfully the issues your child is struggling with, let him know you understand, and offer support and guidance that can gradually empower him to become more at ease socially and personally.

MAKING AND KEEPING FRIENDS

Socially, some gifted kids feel "sidelined" day after day at school. It's fairly common for gifted kids to feel "different" from other kids. The kinds of games your child likes to play, the way she talks, and the things she likes to do, set her apart from many of her peers at school. Some gifted children become loners, avoiding the stress and difficulty of finding other kids like them. The sense of isolation resulting from this is a daily reality for many gifted children, and it can be uncomfortable, even painful.

> I came to school for a meeting and happened to walk by the cafeteria. My daughter was sitting alone with her lunchbox, and I felt so sad. She's such a great kid. Why was she eating by herself? I wondered what I could do to help my lonely child find friends.

Like all kids (and adults), gifted children long to be accepted for who they are. They want the companionship they see other kids enjoying. For some children, the yearning for friendship and acceptance is so strong that they suppress their talents to fit in better with a peer group.

It's hard to see your child struggling to make friends. The truth is, it *is* possible for gifted children to be who they are and still get along with other kids. Here are some ways you can help:

1. **Talk about it.** Listen to find out what your child is experiencing and feeling. As with other difficult situations, it may help to share any struggles you've had, particularly as a child, in making friends or maintaining relationships. Read stories together about friendship. Discuss what makes a good friend; offer your insights frankly and thoughtfully.

2. **Help your child develop social skills.** Some gifted kids grow impatient with people who may not be as quick as they are. Others, accustomed to lots of dialogue with adults, unintentionally come across as superior. There are also gifted children who can be bossy, insisting on organizing every game and running the show. Be alert to signs that your child needs to learn how to cooperate, take turns, and let others into the limelight. Offer to role-play different situations with your child so she can practice friendly give-and-take.

3. **Emphasize what your child has in common with others.** Your child may feel more different than she really is. Yes, she's gifted, but she's like other kids in many ways. Try to find a balance between focusing on her abilities and drawing out traits (like kindness, concern for others, a sense of fun) that will help your child reach toward others in friendship.

4. **Look for ways your child can get to know others who share her interests.** For example, if your child loves animals, see if she could attend a program for kids at the humane society or zoo. She might strike up a friendship with someone there.

5. **Help your child meet other gifted kids, too.** You might start by asking the teacher or gifted education coordinator at school to introduce you to other parents of gifted children. Many parent groups sponsor social events for families. Your child will feel less alone if she knows there are other children like her—kids who may have trouble fitting in at school or sustaining friendships outside of school.

6. **Think broadly about peer groups.** Your child's true peers may be older than she is. Help your child see that it's fine to have several peer groups: kids her own age, kids with her interests, kids on her intellectual level. She will benefit from the experience of interacting with all kinds of people.

TEASING

Gifted children can be especially susceptible to social pressures. Girls, for example, may downplay their talents to avoid drawing attention to themselves. Children whose first language isn't English may keep quiet rather than embarrass themselves in front of classmates by speaking awkwardly.

A child may underachieve to avoid being separated from her friends by being placed in the gifted program. No child is immune from the pressure to conform.

Acute awareness of others and sensitivity to disapproval can magnify a child's feelings of isolation. A gifted student who is teased or scorned for being a "nerd," "brain," or "teacher's pet" often concludes that there's something wrong with her. For many gifted children, being teased is a serious issue. If your child is being teased or bullied:

- **Talk about what's happening.** Listen carefully to your child's concerns and acknowledge how much it hurts to be teased. Ask questions to find out who's doing the teasing and why your child thinks it's happening. Guide your child to look at options: "What do you think might happen if you told this person how you feel?" "What might happen if you don't speak up?" Also talk about why people tease: they may feel jealous or unsure of themselves or think teasing is fun.

- **Help your child plan how to respond.** Depending on the situation, it might be appropriate for your child to walk away, to tell the person "I don't like to be teased—please stop," or to talk to the teacher. If the teasing doesn't stop, you'll need to consult the teacher about it yourself. A child doesn't have to tolerate teasing or bullying. Steps can be taken to correct or change the problem. It shouldn't be ignored.

ANXIETIES AND WORRIES

The heightened sensitivities of a gifted child can lead to anxieties. Your child may be capable of perceiving a great deal about people and situations but too young to articulate what he understands or to put things in perspective. Unusual empathy makes gifted children especially sensitive to difficult situations—divorce, a struggling family member, a sick or dying pet—and to the many forms of thoughtlessness or hostility they may witness at school or on television. Often these children feel helpless to act, which can lead them to criticize themselves for situations they feel responsible for solving. An exceptional imagination can further compound a child's anxieties. A gifted child may project a whole array of troubling scenarios and worry about them intensely:

- One mother described how her eighth-grade son would become tense and worried about upcoming tests. The boy's high level of stress kept him from enjoying anything for several days before an exam.

- A father tells of a child who had great empathy for animals and seemed to suffer when she saw or heard of animals being mal-treated or kept in cages for long periods of time.

- Another parent tells of a child who would cry when he read or watched news stories about starvation and who worried at length about toxic pollution and the shrinking ozone layer.

Take care not to make your child think that what he's feeling is unreasonable or immature—or that it's pointless for him to worry. Rather, respond compassionately and reassuringly:

- "I can see you're really worried about your science test. You know, I also get anxious when I have to write up a report about how one of my projects is going." Tell your child what you do to cope, step-by-step, with your feelings. Gifted children are relieved to know that the adults they admire have concerns just as they do and that it's possible to go beyond distress and take positive steps to face troubling issues. Talk together about ways your child can prepare, mentally and physically, for tests, as well as ways to move his focus away from tests more of the time.

- "I know you feel keenly about how animals are treated. There are places, though, that are committed to better lives for dogs, cats, and other animals. Maybe you and I could volunteer to help at the animal shelter on Saturday mornings. If you'd like, I can check into it." It's important to show your child a way to transform emotional sensitivity into involvement that helps and heals the animals—and her own painful feelings.

- "Our synagogue has a program where a family can help a child who needs food and clothing by sending money and keeping in touch by writing letters. Let's look into it." "Why don't we get on the computer at the library and find out what's being done to help deal with air pollution." It can be devastating for a sensitive child to feel there are no answers for problems like hungry children or a threatened environmental balance. Encouraging your child to gain knowledge and find concrete ways to make a difference shows him he can channel his compassion into constructive action.

Nothing increases a child's anxiety more than the belief that no one understands what he's going through. Like all children, gifted children need adults who can assure them that their concerns, however dramatically expressed, are legitimate—and that they don't need to be immobilized by them.

Nine-year-old Angela was very nervous about having to do a class presentation. She didn't have many friends in the class and thought the other students would laugh at her or whisper while she spoke. She and her father talked about the situation. He told Angela, "When I had stage fright in school, I used to imagine that the class was a bunch of little mice sitting there. If anyone giggled or whispered, it was just a small mouse sniffing the air or twitching its tail." Angela smiled at this and asked, "Did thinking of the kids as mice stop your stage fright?" "No," her dad replied. "What it did was help me laugh inside. You know," he went on, "you used to be afraid of what was in your closet after the lights went out at night. Do you remember how we had to check out the closet before you could turn out the light and go to sleep? Eventually, you got over being afraid of the dark closet. I'll bet you can get over being afraid of giving this report, too."

Angela's father shared with Angela another story and tip about getting through presentations. Once, as a child, he had to recite a poem in front of the class. He practiced the night before in front of his stuffed animals. When he did his presentation the next day, he pictured his animals watching him. That made him feel much better. "It reminded me that I wasn't 'on trial'" he explained. "I didn't have to impress anyone—I just had to recite my poem clearly." Angela liked her dad's idea. She practiced her report in front of her favorite stuffed animals and dolls. Doing this made her feel more confident and gave her images to remember when she did her actual presentation.

This parent used three effective techniques for helping his daughter overcome her fears:

1. He empathized with his daughter by sharing similar fears he had as a child and telling her how he got through them. This showed by example that talking about things that scare or bother us isn't a sign of failure or weakness. It also showed her that he once struggled as she's struggling now. He got through it, and she can, too.

2. He offered his daughter a different way to think about the challenging situation. Instead of seeing it as a big scary event, he helped her use humor to lighten the load.

3. He reminded his daughter of a fear she used to have, but got over. Gifted children, with their vivid imagination and exceptional memory for detail, can easily recall how they used to feel. It's helpful to remind your child that she's overcome fears before, and can do so again—that she can cope and go past being "stuck" on the fear.

What About Your Child?

Angela's father's techniques are useful to keep in mind when helping your child cope with worry and anxiety. Ask yourself:

• What was I afraid of when I was a child? How did I cope with my fears?

• What's easier now for my child than it once was?

• What perspectives could I share with my child to reassure her and help her get past the fear of failure or personal rejection?

Share these ideas with your child.

HELPING YOUR CHILD SHARE FEELINGS

Because of the high standards they often hold for themselves, gifted children sometimes suppress their fears and concerns rather than admit to a perceived weakness. You may need to look for creative ways to encourage your child to share his worries and work through them with you. Try one of these strategies:

• When you're doing some activity with your child, casually bring up school and ask how it's going. A child who's reluctant to talk about his troubles may loosen up while going for a walk or playing a game with you.

• Ask open-ended questions like, "If you could change anything you wanted to in your life, what would you change?" or "If you could solve any problem by waving a magic wand, what problem would you solve?" Encourage your child to answer by saying first what you yourself would change or solve.

• Take your child for an outing. Give him the opportunity to have your undivided attention. You may find yourself having a great conversation. As one parent said, "I feel like I know my child better since we started going out for breakfast together on Saturdays."

Some children benefit from expressing their thoughts and feelings through art or a story. Consider your child's special talents. How can they help him? As appropriate, encourage your child to try one of the following:

• **Create a story** with you about a character who, for example, is teased, is afraid to talk in class, or has a pet that has died. Stories work particularly well for young gifted children who may not be able to discuss how they feel but who can make the connection between a story and themselves.

- **Keep a journal** for writing about what excites, exhilarates, frightens, or troubles your child. Journaling provides a wonderful forum for young people to reflect, analyze, and strategize about things that concern them.

- **Seek out books about characters who face various difficult situations.** Ask a librarian to guide you to books about specific themes or challenges. You might read the book, too, or read it with your child, so you can talk together about how individuals cope with problems. If the book is a work of fiction, you could also discuss other ways the book might have ended or a character might have behaved.

- **With a young child, use a puppet to express feelings.** Children who have trouble talking directly about what's bothering them can sometimes confide through the mouth of a puppet.

- **Together, create a skit or do a role play about a troubling situation.** Ask your child which role he'd like you to play.

- **Encourage your child to use the creative arts**—writing, dance, drama, storytelling, singing, drawing, sculpting—to show how he'd like life to be. Have him convey through art a near-perfect school, the friends he'd like to have, his ideal home or bedroom, the places he'd like to visit, and so on. Often, such creations will suggest parts of life that trouble your child or make him unhappy.

- **Read biographies as a way to envision the future.** All children, including gifted children, have a difficult time seeing beyond the present. Learning about the childhoods of distinguished men and women can be inspirational. Gifted children find it strengthening to read about the lives of others and the adversities they had to meet as part of growing up.

The Power of Biography: Find Out More

Stories of accomplished people from diverse backgrounds who failed many times, suffered setbacks, and endured the disapproval of others without giving up can provide powerful role models for gifted kids. Here are three places to look for interesting biographies:

National Women's History Project
7738 Bell Road
Windsor, CA 95492-8518
1-800-691-8888
www.nwhp.org
The finest publisher of biographies on women of all nationalities and cultures offers a splendid collection of books, materials, and games for children.

Libby Hughes is an author who has written diverse biographies for young adults. Some of her subjects include Nelson Mandela, Margaret Thatcher, Christopher Reeve, Colin Powell, Tiger Woods, and more. Check out her biographies at your local library or book store.

KidsClick!
sunsite.berkeley.edu/KidsClick!
A search engine for kids designed by librarians. Visit the home page and click on Biography under the Geography/History/Biography section for a list of more than 60 biography sites for children. Includes many sites focused on African-Americans.

Show your child that he can use his abilities as resources for coping. Gifted kids can make extraordinary mental leaps and are capable of complex thinking. They enjoy tackling difficult problems. Their strong sense of justice and fairness can help them see things from a variety of perspectives. It takes imagination and original thinking to overcome life's challenges. By reminding your child of his capabilities, you can help him build strategies for handling his concerns.

As your child's advocate, the best gift you can impart is support that leads him to be his *own* advocate. Gifted kids with a strong sense of their own identity have fewer emotional problems and an easier time getting along with other children. The more they realize there's nothing wrong (and a lot that's *right*) with having special strengths and sensitivities, the less they will censure themselves and the more freedom they will feel to be themselves.

OVERCOMING PERFECTIONISM

Gifted children all too easily feel pressured *because* of their abilities. They may want instant results, steady progress at all times. When these don't happen, they may begin to doubt themselves. Because they're still children, their advanced intellectual ability often exceeds their physical skills and emotional maturity. When this uneven development doesn't allow them to achieve the way they want to, they can become frustrated and impatient with themselves. They may also hide the gaps in their knowledge, feel nervous about asking for help because they think they should know everything, and worry obsessively about pleasing the people who admire them.

A gifted musician described some trouble she ran into because of her ability to play by ear. The adults assumed she was reading music and when she protested that she couldn't do so, they would contradict her: "Of course you can—don't say that!" So she concluded that she *should* be able to read music, and this was the start of a negative pattern in her life. She began to feel pressure to *know* without the process that knowledge demands. The adults around her unwittingly robbed her of the learning she needed.

In the classroom, perfectionism can arise if a child is far beyond her classmates in ability. Such a child ties her achievement in school to her worth as a person. Frequently, the standards the child holds inside far exceed those of her parent or teachers. So, even if a parent or teacher says, "This is excellent. You don't need to do any more on this," the child won't believe it. Perfectionism may also be part of what plagues an underachieving gifted child, who may have convinced herself that it's better to attempt little and slide by than to try hard and possibly fail.

Often, perfectionism is a family affair. We parents, with the best of motivations, may unintentionally feed perfectionism when we expect straight A's and consistently excellent school performance. A child will feel and internalize this pressure, whether it's spoken or not. The high expectations of the adults around them can make gifted children severe judges of themselves and their work. They may become fixated on extrinsic rewards (such as grades and praise) rather than intrinsic rewards (the joy of learning). They may value only the final product, rather than the all-important process.

You may wonder, don't I want my child to live up to her potential? Isn't it my job to help her do this? The answer is yes—as long as you don't confuse striving for excellence with a quest for perfection. Perfectionism sets an impossible standard. A perfectionistic child believes she can *never* fail, must *constantly* do the absolute best and most, should *always* receive praise and approval. Excellence is a very different standard. A child who strives for excellence can feel free to take risks and try new things. She knows that she needn't always excel—that sometimes, in fact, she'll fail.

What About Your Child?

Use this quick inventory to help you recognize signs of perfectionism. Does your child usually or often:

- Avoid trying new things for fear of failure?
- Procrastinate, fret over details, and leave work unfinished (or never start it) out of fear it won't be good enough?
- Focus on mistakes, rather than on what was done well?
- Set unrealistic goals and then condemn herself when she doesn't achieve them?
- Have trouble accepting criticism?
- Find it hard to laugh at herself?
- Focus on end products, rather than on the process of learning?
- Avoid learning situations that may involve risk and the possibility of low grades?
- Judge herself severely whenever she gets anything below an A?
- Underachieve in preference to attempting and possibly failing?
- Appear to love learning less and less because she's convinced she'll never reach some impossibly high standard?

If you answered yes to several of these questions, perfectionism may be a problem for your child.

Be aware of the expectations you may have created for your gifted child. Ask yourself: Are my expectations reasonable? Am I allowing my child the freedom to be herself, express herself, have fun, fool around, make mistakes—be a child? With patience and understanding, you can guide your son or daughter away from perfectionism. Here are some ways to get started:

1. **Show your child that you love and accept her for who she is,** that your love is independent of what she does or achieves. Express at least as much appreciation of her interests and individuality (what makes her special) as of her achievements (high grades and awards).

2. **Help your child set realistic goals.** Show her how to break large projects into small, manageable steps. Reassure her that learning gaps can be addressed, and help her recognize when she's expecting too much of herself.

3. **Let your child know that mistakes are okay,** that everyone makes them, and that they're part of the learning process. Acknowledge your own mistakes.

4. **Teach your child the value of patience**—with herself and with the process of learning. Convey to her that it's safe to make mistakes and be imperfect in the relaxed environment of home.

5. **Remind your child that nobody's perfect** and nobody's good at everything—not her and not you.

6. **Applaud your child's efforts.** Encourage *process* over product—what she *learns* rather than what she accomplishes or produces.

7. **Celebrate creativity**—the unusual or innovative response to an assignment or question—rather than the "right" answer.

8. **Use praise discerningly.** Don't lavish praise on your child for excelling or dwell on her achievements, especially in her presence. You can express joy in her successes without making her feel that these accomplishments alone are what make her special or define her identity. Don't praise every little thing your child says or does. Children who are praised all the time start believing that what they do is more important than who they are. Believing this, they may be unable to accept any praise, since nothing they do meets their own impossible standards.

9. **Point out positive actions that have nothing to do with ability.** Commend your child for taking risks, even when things don't turn out the way she planned. Focus on efforts as well as successes. Notice appropriate ways of handling failure and thoughtful interactions with other people.

10. **Involve your child in activities that aren't graded or judged.** Invite her to try things "just for fun." Encourage her to spend more time doing what she loves to do—taking walks, reading mysteries or science fiction, playing with the dog, or playing board games with friends or siblings.

11. **Help your child plan for challenges.** When your child is about to start something new, talk with her about what might go wrong and what she'll do if that happens.

12. **Help your child choose what does and doesn't call for her best effort.** Which things require the greatest investment of time and energy? Which things simply need to be finished—to be "good enough"?

13. **Encourage your child's sense of humor.** Help her lighten up about things that don't go her way.

14. **If your child doesn't like what she did, help her see why.** Don't dismiss her feelings ("What do you mean you don't like your poster? It's wonderful!"). Listen to what she says and help her explore how she might do things differently in the future. ("Do you think you could do more sketching in pencil next time, before you paint?")

15. **Turn your child's attention away from flaws in her work** and toward what she has learned and accomplished. You might say, "You've told me you're disappointed with some parts of your project. Now tell me what's good about what you've done."

16. **Take a look at your own perfectionist qualities.** Are you too hard on yourself? Are you setting for your child the example you want to set—of someone who enjoys his own achievements and doesn't criticize himself all the time for not doing better?

There's a big difference between wanting your child to develop her potential and wanting her to be tops at everything she tries. When you're clear that inner achievement—the development of high-level thinking skills, the extension of creative imagination, the ability to take risks, the joy of discovery—is far more important than high grades and awards, you'll be able to help your child combat perfectionism.

Perfectionism: Find Out More

Perfectionism: What's Bad About Being Too Good? (Revised and Updated Edition) by Miriam Adderholdt, Ph.D., and Jan Goldberg (Minneapolis: Free Spirit Publishing, 1999). Though written for teenagers, this book gives adults valuable insights into how their behavior and expectations can contribute to perfectionism in their kids.

WHEN LISTENING, GUIDING, AND ENCOURAGING AREN'T ENOUGH

If your efforts to help your child cope with fears, anxieties, or perfectionism don't seem to be working, it may be time to seek professional help. Ask yourself these questions:

- Does my child continue to seem unduly concerned about the opinions of other kids at school?

- Has there been a sudden drop in my child's school performance or a lessening of interest in things he used to love?

- Has my child's behavior changed abruptly? Is he spending much more time alone? Is he much less communicative than he's been? Am I getting reports of misbehavior at school that don't sound typical of my child?

- Is my child having physical problems when it's time to go to school, such as headaches and nervousness?

- When I talk to my child about things he fears, does he get very dramatic, explaining in vivid detail what he imagines might happen? Or is he unable to explain what he's feeling?

- Does my child feel intimidated in school, unsure of expressing his opinions, afraid of what others might think, disinclined to pursue his interests as he does at home?

- Does my child show acute frustration when he can't shape his ideas the way he would like to? Does he have tantrums or slam doors?

- Is my child moody? Do his moods swing from one extreme to another?

If you're concerned about your child's mental health, don't hesitate to enlist the support of a counselor, learning specialist, school psychologist, pediatrician, social worker, or clergyperson.

Supporting Emotional Needs: Find Out More

Here's an organization that helps parents and children understand and accept the unique talents of gifted children. It also provides a forum for parents and educators to connect and communicate about living and working with gifted kids:

Supporting the Emotional Needs of the Gifted (SENG)
P.O. Box 6550
Scottsdale, AZ 85261
(602) 399-9090
www.sengifted.org

Helping gifted children navigate a sometimes scary, often intense emotional terrain takes work. It's worth the effort. Supporting your child—in whatever way you find you need to—can lead to lifelong rewards for both of you.

> My parents are still my best friends. When I was a kid, I'd often come home from school upset and discouraged. I'd go to my parents, and we'd talk it through. Sometimes we'd figure out a way to solve the problem—sometimes I had to just put up with it. But I never felt alone. So even now, when I'm stressed and can't figure out what to do, I call my parents. By the time we're done talking, I feel the same way I did as a kid. I think, "I can do this. It'll be okay."

Take a Stand!

Perfectionism is a pervasive issue for many gifted children. Take some time to consider whether your child is struggling with this challenge. Start by making an honest inventory of your expectations for your child, considering whether you're setting the stage for perfectionism. Next think about your child, answering the questions in "What About Your Child?" (page 43). Then, referring to the ideas on pages 43–45, identify two or three specific things you can start doing now to help your child move away from perfectionism. If you wish, use the notebook you started in Chapter 2 to keep track of your observations, the steps you take, and how you see your child responding.

Chapter 4
Advocacy Is . . .
Guiding Your Child with Helpful Discipline

I sometimes wonder if we're overindulging our highly gifted, highly verbal son, Jeffrey. I find myself trying to reason with him like he's 25 instead of 10, especially when he's doing something he's not supposed to—but treating him like an adult doesn't work! I get into these long talks with Jeffrey about his behavior, and sometimes he really puts me on the defensive. The problem is, when you have a sensitive kid who talks and reasons like someone so much older, it's hard to discipline him.

Becky, our youngest, is always testing her limits—and ours. When she was three I saw her beginning to bury her sandwich in this large hole she'd dug. I was about to yell when I stopped myself and just asked her what she was doing. She answered, "I'm storing my food for the winter!" Now she's seven. Yesterday I found her busy mixing peanut butter with flour, sugar, and uncooked rice. She looked at me casually and asked, "Dad, do you think the rice will cook if I bake these cookies? Or will it be as hard as it is now?" Becky's teacher tells us Becky is messy, never pays attention, and is always doing something other than her schoolwork. My wife and I have argued about how to handle this unusual child. She thinks Becky needs strict rules about her behavior and schoolwork, with consequences if she doesn't do what she's supposed to do. I'm afraid too much discipline will put a damper on her creativity and imagination.

As a teacher and a parent, I almost dislike the term *discipline* in relation to gifted kids, yet the reality is that gifted kids do need discipline. We do them a disservice when we don't establish expectations and limits. But what kind of expectations? What type of limits?

The origin of the word *discipline* comes from the Latin *discere*, which means *to learn*. In this sense, discipline is teaching. Disciplining gifted children means helping them learn to be responsible, honest, sensitive, and caring. It's balance that we're talking about, a combination of love and principle. With this kind of guidance, your child's gifts have all the more room to flourish because she knows there's someone there to keep her on the right path. Over time, helpful discipline can also support your child in getting along with friends, teachers, and peers.

Discipline can seem a complicated matter for a child you want desperately not to discourage—particularly if she's frustrated and bored in school. Your child's sophisticated thinking, imagination, and vocabulary may lead you to believe, consciously or unconsciously, that she's more mature than she really is—more able to handle things on her own. Yet, as intelligent as they may be, gifted kids are children first: young, lacking insight and experience, with much to learn in order to become responsible adults. A child treated as if she's much older may start to make unreasonable demands on herself, and this can lead to guilt or self-condemnation and a loss of self-esteem. I have seen the tense faces of gifted children who believe they should be more adult than they are. Such children may think they must stifle their childlike feelings.

Often, parents don't realize they may be assuming too much emotional maturity in their child. A parent once told me of being brought up short one day in the midst of her daughter's tantrum. When the mother cried in frustration, "You're acting like a little kid!" the child shouted back, "Mom, I *am* a little kid!"

THE IMPORTANCE OF LIMITS

All children need and want limits. They want to feel that someone cares enough about them to say no and mean it. Without limits, kids don't feel safe or protected enough to develop their interests and talents. There's a difference between giving your child *freedom* and giving him *license*—tacit permission—to do whatever he wants. Every child needs the freedom to explore, learn, and pursue things he loves. In this sense, there's no such thing as too much freedom. But you *can* give your child too much license, to the point where he assumes that your main job is to meet all his wants and wishes.

What Happens When There Are No Limits?

It's not just a question of becoming spoiled. With little or no parental guidance, children will soon run into problems. A child from a too-permissive home will have trouble coping with the demands of school—the need to get along with others, to endure occasional disappointments, and to persist in working hard even when rewards aren't forthcoming. A lax style of upbringing can be stressful for any child, but it's all the more so for a gifted child whose heightened sensibilities can compound the duress. Unaccustomed to rules and limits, a child may:

- **Lack resourcefulness.** When things don't go his way, he may become completely dependent on someone bailing him out.

- **Be unable to accept correction or guidance.** Because he's never had anyone rein him in, he may believe that adults do not or cannot know what's best for him.

- **Feel anxious and inadequate.** A child who has little structure at home sometimes concludes that he *should* be able to handle everything in his life alone. When he can't, he worries.

- **Lack flexibility.** A child may find it very difficult to compromise or negotiate with others.

- **Misbehave.** A child who hasn't had enough parental input on what he can and can't do may become disruptive.

A Balancing Act

When you establish, communicate, and enforce clear limits for behavior, you give your child the safety of knowing how his family environment works and what his place is in it. Your child needs some routine and structure in his life. Again, balance is the key—knowing *when* to set limits, and *what kind.* The parameters you set create a framework for the survival of everyone in the family. There are areas of family life where a child can make choices and participate in decisions; there are others where you need to decide. Even in the little things—mealtimes, bedtimes, chores—you may want some established practices that aren't negotiated every day, if only for your own sanity!

It's essential that your child understand and accept your authority as his parent. This doesn't mean you'll dominate or oppress him. But you can't protect, guide, and prepare your gifted child for the outside world if there's confusion about leadership roles at home. It's equally important that you skillfully assert your authority as a parent when your child tests the boundaries, something gifted children may do *more* than other children. Your child is exploring the terrain of your relationship—the things that are okay, the things that aren't. If you back off from your parental role, your child will come to expect others to do as he wants, accommodate his needs, agree with him, and give him a great deal of attention. The standard you want to set is one of mutual respect.

In guiding your child, approach the setting of limits as an expression of your love. Explain rules and limits to your child from that vantage point. She won't always understand or accept why she can't do what she wants. She'll apply her reasoning ability to what you say and try to argue with you. It's okay, sometimes, to say, "You'll have to trust me on this. It's not safe. You can't do it, and that's that." You don't need to have a long discussion about everything. In fact, your child needs to know that some rules are nonnegotiable.

Parenting experts offer a variety of strategies for disciplining children without punishing or spoiling them. Some of these strategies include:

- **Listening** to what's going on from your child's point of view.

- **Using nonjudgmental language** to explain what worries you or how you feel without blaming or escalating a situation: "When I hear you bossing your friends, I worry that they won't want to play with you." "Yelling at me isn't acceptable. After you calm down, we can talk about it."

- **Respecting both your child *and* yourself** as you set limits.

- **Setting consequences that fit the situation.** Yelling, spanking, and grounding kids are not helpful consequences. They may stop misbehavior for a while, but the message to the child is that violence and excessive power are acceptable ways to deal with problems. Keeping in mind the purpose of discipline—to teach, guide, and encourage self-discipline—will help you apply constructive consequences. You want your child to grow in taking responsibility for herself.

- **Giving children a voice—and a choice—**whenever possible. Many times, children can help decide limits and consequences. This mutual approach is important in fostering honest and fair communication.

- **Establishing family rules.** Children thrive in families that establish together certain principles or rules that everyone knows are important. They learn that in certain areas their parents make the decisions. They also discover that in some areas *they* can help decide—their feelings and perceptions as contributing family members are taken into account. It's always advisable, whenever possible, to create rules that everyone in the family understands and agrees to.

Many gifted children have a strong sense of justice and injustice and expect the family's standards to apply to everyone. Your child may speak up when she thinks a sibling, or *you*, have fallen short of a family principle. One boy, whose mother objected to his being at friends' homes all day and never staying home with the family, pointed out that Mom frequently worked weekends. "If we have to be home part of the time, then you should be too, Mom," he said. The mother realized that she'd better look closely at her schedule.

Your child needs to know that she does have a voice in some family decisions, that her opinions are valued, and that she can influence family life in positive ways. If you want your gifted child to share her belongings with her brother or sister more readily, for example, let her participate in creating some guidelines about getting along with others. Allowing her to help formulate rules gives her an opportunity to use her abilities in a constructive way.

Just as an important goal of your advocacy is to enable your child to take charge of her own learning, a key objective of your parenting is to help your child learn self-discipline and responsibility. Your integrity and consistency set the stage for your child to mature. You don't want to stifle your child by exerting control over everything she does, nor do you want to leave her without a realistic sense of boundaries. Balance is both the framework and the goal.

Discipline and Parenting: Find Out More

Mary Sheedy Kurcinka has written books that are especially helpful for parents of gifted kids:

Kids, Parents, and Power Struggles: Winning for a Lifetime (New York: HarperCollins, 2000). The author builds on Daniel Goleman's concept of emotional intelligence to offer creative techniques for using power struggles as pathways to better understanding within the family.

Raising Your Spirited Child: A Guide for Parents Whose Child Is More Intense, Sensitive, Perceptive, Persistent, Energetic (New York: HarperCollins, 1992). Reframing challenging temperamental qualities ("difficult") in a positive way ("spirited"), Kurcinka offers tools for parents to better understand and enjoy their child. Also check out the *Raising Your Spirited Child Workbook* (New York: HarperCollins, 1998).

FINDING THE TIME

Like many parents, you may worry that you're not spending enough time with your child. The demands of work, family commitments, and household chores can eat up a parent's waking hours.

I'm a single parent with two gifted kids, a second grader and a fifth grader. I work long hours, and I'm afraid my kids resent my not having much time for them. They hate it that I'm not around when they get home from school. I'm especially worried about my son. He's very sensitive and impressionable, and I don't like some of the kids he's been spending time with. They're not interested in school. Before my divorce I worked part-time and was able to supervise his work and get him involved in things he liked to do, like taking guitar lessons. What do I do now to make sure he does worthwhile things and doesn't feel intimidated by other kids? How can I find time to give him the attention he needs from me?

In our fragmented, intensive lives, carving out family time can be a formidable challenge. Yet it's essential that you find a way to spend time with your gifted child. You may have to go about this creatively. Start by looking at your schedule for the week and setting some new priorities. Maybe you can make a "date" with your child—a time to go somewhere together, eat together, or do something active that you both enjoy. If you have chores or errands that can't be neglected, why not do some of these in partnership with your child? Gifted children, especially in families with more than one child, treasure "alone time" with a parent. I used to reserve Friday afternoon or evening for this private time with my own daughter.

Enlist your child's help in finding time to spend together. Gifted children tend to be very sensitive and can understand a great deal more than we expect. Problems arise when we struggle with the issue privately and say nothing. You might say: "Look, I have lots of things I need to do but I want to make sure I'm here for you when you need me and that we spend some good time together. What would you like us to do? Let's set up some special time just for you and me."

Besides "special" time, set aside a part of every day to devote to your child. This might be first thing in the morning, before or after dinner, or before bed. Find some quiet time when your child can talk about his day, show you what he's working on, or read or draw with you.

I've started two daily rituals with my son Leth. Every day after work, weather permitting, we go outside for a game of catch. You'd be amazed at the discussions we get into just tossing a ball back and forth. Leth finds it easier to talk about things while we're doing something else, rather than just face-to-face. For our second daily ritual, I lie down with Leth at bedtime to continue a story we started together about two years ago. It's about an adventurous amphibian named Max. We must have about a hundred episodes by now. I start the story off, he fleshes it out, I throw in a surprise twist, he throws in another, and so on. At first, it was just a lure to get him to go to bed. Now it's become something we do together and enjoy. We both have fun letting our imaginations run wild.

The time this parent actually spends with his son isn't particularly long, but they do at least two fun things together every day. That's important. When you make time for your gifted child, you don't have to think of hours. Think of minutes. Think of little rituals that can help knit your relationship and show your child he's an important part of your life.

When my daughter Felicia started middle school, I noticed we'd stopped doing much together. She used to love baking cookies, so I got her involved fixing supper with me. Felicia grumbled at first, but pretty soon she got into it in a big way. For her, cooking is like science, her favorite subject. While we worked, we talked about ingredients and their properties. Felicia was also intrigued with the whole process of meal planning and preparation. Sometimes, she'd plan a special meal for the family. We'd create a menu together, thinking through what flavors would blend well. This routine of fixing supper really helped connect us. Now we're starting to do more things together—other chores like cleaning and shopping, but also fun stuff like reading, doing art and science projects, visiting museums, and going inline skating. I've found I enjoy being with Felicia so much that it hasn't been as hard as I thought it would be to find time for her!

Think about areas of your life that you could rearrange to make more time for your child. Could you negotiate at work for the opportunity to leave early once in a while? Some employers are sensitive to parents' needs and may, for example, allow you to switch to a different shift, start work early and come home early, work through your lunch period so you can get an afternoon off once a week, or work at home one or two days a week to save you travel time. It may even be possible to cut back on your work hours or let certain home chores go for a while so you can carve out an extra half-hour here and there.

If you have a spouse or partner, look carefully at ways the two of you can become more of a childrearing team. If you both have weekends off, plan regular family activities for Saturday or Sunday. You might take turns leaving work early to be home when your child returns from school. Be sure that whichever parent is gone the most in a day gets special time with the child in the evening. If you're a single parent, try teaming up with a close friend or relative to spend time with your child and hers.

Time spent with your child now is an investment in his future and yours. You'll be establishing a pattern that will help keep communication open for years to come.

Take a Stand!

Many parents have regular family meetings where all members can talk about whatever's on their mind. Starting routine meetings can be an ideal way to involve children in decision making and to talk over any conflicts, misjudgments, rivalries, or misunderstandings. Why not give family meetings a try? Make a commitment to having meetings once a week for the next month. At each meeting, talk first about what's going well in the family. Then work together to develop household rules, solve problems, and plan something fun to do.

Family Meetings: Find Out More

The Parent's Handbook by Don Dinkmeyer Sr., Gary D. McKay, and Don Dinkmeyer Jr. (Circle Pines, MN: American Guidance Service, 1997). This book gives simple but useful guidelines for establishing regular family meetings that help families work together. It also discusses democratic parenting, reflective listening, "I-messages," logical consequences, and ways to encourage and affirm children.

Chapter 5
Advocacy Is . . .
Providing a Haven for Learning

One rainy day I was home with my two kids. I proposed that we put on a puppet show, which I would videotape. I've never seen my kids so excited—my daughter even told a friend who called that she was busy and couldn't play! We found some small paper bags, and the kids painted faces on them. While they worked, they created the plot for their show. I had to intervene once or twice when arguments flared up, but the kids worked furiously all day creating the characters, rehearsing their scenes, and then practicing with their puppets on a table (which they used as a stage). I videotaped one practice, and the kids were surprised to discover that their heads poked up above the table several times. They asked me to tape them again. Later, after my wife got home, they performed their show for us. What a great day!

You are your child's first teacher—and the most accurate judge of her ability. If, like many parents of gifted children, you were besieged by questions and requests for information as soon as your child could talk, you probably became a teacher almost by default. This role doesn't end because your child is in school. You have a large, vital part to play in your child's education. Part of discovering your power as a parent advocate is embracing your power to consistently enrich your child's learning when she's *not* in school.

In many of the world's cultures, parents never question their right or qualifications to teach their own children. They simply know that, as parents, it's their job to impart to their children what they know—a body of knowledge, deep spiritual truths, a set of survival skills, and a capacity to solve problems. Regardless of the learning opportunities provided at school, you have much to offer your child. Your home can become a place where your child not only feels nurtured and supported, but also can grow as a learner and a maturing, caring individual.

Being a parent who creates fun, memorable learning opportunities in and around your home may demand a new view of yourself. Maybe you've doubted your capacity to provide stimulation and challenge suitable for your child's exceptional abilities. You don't need a college degree or a special interest in math or science to support your child's learning. You don't need to own a piano, a telescope, a camera, a stereo system, or a computer either—though it's great if you do. Whatever your education, whatever your income, there are opportunities for enrichment and challenge outside the classroom that only *you* can provide. It's less important *how* you choose to get involved in your child's learning than *that* you do it.

LEARNING IN AND AROUND YOUR HOME

In making your home a creative, challenging place for your child, everyday things can be valuable teaching aids. Newspapers, books, magazines, maps, tools, recipes, Legos, dolls, collections, plants, a family pet, a TV or radio program, music videos, games, and your family's mealtime discussions are all sources of learning. As educator William F. Russell states:

> It is what you do in the course of your normal, everyday family life that determines and creates the attitudes that your children have both toward their schooling and toward learning in general. Is it okay to be curious in your home? Can children ask "why?" about things they see or hear or read without appearing silly or ignorant or meddlesome? Do your children ever hear you wonder aloud when something stimulates your own curiosity, and then watch or accompany you in a search for that missing piece of knowledge?*

Start by Paying Attention

Tune in to your child's interests. Don't minimize the value of family conversations. Sit together and talk with your child—on a picnic, around the table, in the car, on the front stoop. Show her that you're interested in her thoughts and ideas.

For weeks my daughter Keesha had been asking for a model airplane for her birthday. I kept thinking unhappily about a messy project cluttering up the dining room table. But she talked about the model so much that I bought one for her at the last minute. She was ecstatic when she opened the gift, and wanted to start working on the model before we'd even cut the birthday cake! Well, once she'd opened the box and spread some of the pieces around, I started to get interested, too. I asked if I could join her, and she just beamed. We had a great time putting that model together. It took us about two weeks working

---

* *Family Learning: How to Help Your Child Succeed in School by Learning at Home* by William F. Russell, St. Charles, IL: First Word Learning Systems, 1997, page 14.

a little every night. Keesha has a friend who likes models, too, and today she asked if we could start a "model airplane club" with her friend and his dad. It's great to see Keesha so excited about learning—and it's fun to be part of it. Why didn't I pay attention sooner?

By really listening to his daughter, this parent supported her learning in a way that opened up the opportunity for mutual learning and a stronger relationship. From here, there are any number of ways he and his daughter can explore building and airplanes. They might branch out into models of cars, trains, tractors, or space vehicles. They might decide to fly model airplanes, attend air shows, even take flying lessons. Or, they might simply enjoy building model planes together now and again. Keesha may continue to pursue this interest on her own, without her dad's involvement, too. Regardless, by paying attention to his daughter's interests and showing a real interest, this father found a way to capture and build on his child's curiosity. What she'll learn and experience will extend and expand into other areas of her education and her life.

What About Your Child?

Tune in to the variety of things that spark your child's curiosity by listening and watching a little more closely. Does your child:

• Have a favorite TV program she never misses? What's it about? Why does she like it?

• Play certain games again and again? Why does she like them? Does she play them alone? With a sibling or friend?

• Especially enjoy a certain uncle or aunt? What does she like about this relative? What do they talk about and do together? Do they tell jokes? Talk sports? Go on special outings?

• Love animals? Does she have a pet? Beg to go to the zoo? Watch animal specials on TV? Want to learn all she can about a certain kind of animal?

• Like certain books and go back to particular ones as favorites?

Once you identify some of the things that excite your child, ask yourself: What can I do to build on this excitement in learning, this joy of discovering new ideas and possibilities for learning more?

Foster Creativity Through the Arts

Many public schools need to go further in promoting creative thinking across the curriculum. They need to emphasize the arts far more as media for higher-level thinking and self-expression. With budget constraints, creative and fine arts are too often treated as "frills" that can be cut when funding falls short. This is an obvious misinterpretation of the essential place the arts have in enhancing gifted children's (and all children's) growth. It can be a tragedy. Integrating the arts in all subjects can advance immeasurably the child's ability to think and delight in learning. Too often, "gifted" is defined by parents and teachers alike as solely the academic or intellectual. Inventing, imagining, and expressing ideas through the arts can sharpen a gifted child's thinking in all disciplines.

When you involve your child in artistic expression—whether it be painting, collage, music, mime, dramatics, or movement—you may be surprised by the enthusiasm these activities generate. And artistic activities don't always need planning. "Serendipity"—or the joy of discovery—is inherent in a child's involvement in the arts. Creative moments can occur at any time in your day and demand just a little extra energy to exploit. They can often occur spontaneously:

- If it's fall and the leaves in your neighborhood are changing color, you and your child could go out to collect leaves. Back at home, you could encourage your child to draw the ones he collected in careful detail or to write a free-verse poem as a response to what he's just seen outdoors.

- If you're preparing a meal, you could invite your child to write up a fancy menu or create placecards.

- If you're headed across town on the bus or train, start a story with your child about some of the people you see around you, with each of you adding to it as you go.

- If you're listening to music, make a tape or burn a CD of favorite songs from a wide variety of music genres and eras.

Many gifted children want the opportunity to "make something new," and art is a process of making. Artistic self-expression, even when done casually, places your child in the position of inventor and creator. So much of education focuses on repeating and reiterating. Gifted children may be starved for opportunities to originate and craft, design and develop.

Consider exposing your child to the arts at home. Encourage artistic outlets. Some kids get their best ideas when they leave the problems or homework they're working on to sculpt, paint, play an instrument, listen to music, or dance around the room.

Emily has always been restless when she's working on an idea, and early on I started turning on music to relax her. From a very young age, she'd begin prancing around the living room. She would do these beautiful movements and pantomimes. Now she's eleven, and she still does this. When she's had enough, I find her back at her desk, on the trail of another idea.

Emily is refreshed and recharged by the experience of free, uninhibited movement in safe surroundings. If you've noticed that your child loves movement, consider dance lessons, gymnastics, sports, or dramatics.

Encouraging your child to explore various creative media can help him discover his interests. A fifth grader I know had always done detailed sketches of everything in his home—the kitchen table, a vase, a bookcase, a lamp. His parents took him to museums and to the library for books on various arts and artists. They encouraged him to draw, sculpt, and paint, and he developed a special interest in architecture. In fact, architecture has become the driving force behind his learning. Whenever he has a history project at school, for example, he and his parents seek out books and other information on the architecture of that time. His parents are now exploring the possibility of finding an architect willing to mentor their son. (See pages 126–129 for more on mentorships.)

If your child expresses exceptional talent in the arts and you're able to supply lessons, be discriminating in your choice of teacher. Pay attention to the *kind* of gift your child has and what sort of teacher will best nurture it. Talent can be fragile if it isn't understood and supported. In some instances, you may discover that it's better to leave your child alone to explore and develop independently of formal instruction, at least for a while. As always, trust your own instincts about your child and keep observing his talents and interests.

Do Things As a Family

Whenever possible, explore and learn as a family. Your local library is a ready source of reading material, technology, information, free enrichment programs, and book searches. Go on outings with your child, too. Seek out free or low-cost places to visit: museums, historical sites, the humane society or a veterinary clinic, the post office, a newspaper or magazine office, an apple orchard or a dairy farm, a horse stable, a fire or police station. Visit aquariums, zoos, planetariums, art galleries. When you can, attend plays, concerts, sporting events. Community centers usually offer classes, recreational facilities, and information. Religious organizations often sponsor programs for families and children. Go with your child on organized walks, runs, or biking trips. Whatever you do, keep it fun. Your goal isn't to repli-cate the formal learning environment of a school, but to help your child, and your family, make learning a natural part of everyday living.

Everything you do can become a catalyst for a child's independent proj-ects and spurs to new interests. Your family's stargazing, for example, may awaken your child's interest in astronomy. You could then look together for books on the subject, visit a local observatory, watch a video on space travel, and check the Internet for interesting Web sites. Maybe she'll be motivated to write and illustrate science fiction stories or to develop a book of poetry based on the stars.

Look for Teachable Moments
You can find opportunities every day to turn ordinary events into "teach-able moments"—always keeping that spirit of fun.

When my six-year-old son Reggie and I were shopping, we saw that a certain brand of cookies was half off. Reggie asked me what "half off" meant, and we got into an interesting discussion. I gave him an example: "One half of all your fingers is five fingers. Two groups of five fingers equal the number of all your fingers." Reggie absorbed this information with great interest. Then he said, "So, if you want to get the full price, you add this price twice?" He'd understood the concept just fine.

Instead of giving a quick and easy response ("It means it's on sale" or "I'll explain later"), this parent helped her child understand something he was intrigued by. Time taken to do this is rarely wasted.

I know a parent who volunteered at a nature center. She routinely brought along her son Michael, and he developed a deep interest in ecology there. He and his mother worked together on a local conservation project to reintroduce native prairie plants to a woodland area. Michael read exten-sively on the subject of vanishing prairie plant species and tried a few seeds in his own backyard. Within a year, the family's backyard had become Michael's prairie project! This interest led to opportunities for him to present and display his work at the science fair, as well as write about it for the local paper. There's no way of telling what stimulus, what example, what experi-ence will set in motion this kind of growth and enthusiasm in a gifted learner!

Investigate Enrichment Programs
Weekend, after-school, and summer enrichment programs can offer your child the opportunity to pursue interests and subject matter not usually

offered in school. What does your child like to do? Take nature walks? Do chemistry experiments? Write, direct, or act in plays? Sculpt? Do creative movement? What would your child like to learn about? Law? Architecture? Archaeology? Oceanography? Computer programming? Renaissance art? Investigate the possibilities by checking community newspapers and magazines, getting information from your school, contacting your local or state gifted association, calling the nearest college or university, or talking with other parents in person or on the Internet. You might also contact places that focus on specific subjects or activities, such as art schools, music studios, dance academies, aquariums, museums, community organizations, language programs, cultural associations, libraries, arboretums, ecology centers, zoos, and camps. Many programs offer scholarships, graduated tuition, or special payment plans, so be sure to ask about all of the options.

As you explore various opportunities, be sure to consult with your child about what he'd like to do. All kids need a break from school, so be sensitive to programs that don't sound like much fun. Many enrichment programs, such as those offered at The Center for Gifted at National-Louis University (see page 175), include topics not usually offered in school, such as robotics, journalism, law, creative writing, and filmmaking. They also tend to focus on activities that are project-centered, hands-on, experimental, and investigative. Many gifted kids love to explore new fields and use their talents in an open, ungraded setting where they're free to take greater risks and apply themselves without the usual classroom pressures or limits.

Encouraging Learning: Find Out More

National Association for Gifted Children (NAGC)
1707 L Street NW, Suite 550
Washington, DC 20036
(202) 785-4268
www.nagc.org
NAGC is a national advocacy organization for parents and educators in support of gifted education. Visit the Web site to find a list of state gifted organizations. A subscription to the quarterly magazine *Parenting for High Potential* is a benefit of NAGC membership. NAGC and your state gifted association can tell you about organizations and associations (including universities) in your area that offer programs. The NAGC Web site lists summer and enrichment programs and special schools, and reprints of two articles, "How to Choose a Summer Program" and "Questions to Ask When Researching a Summer Camp."

Gifted Canada
www3.telus.net/giftedcanada
This Web site posts contacts for an array of organizations and topics related to gifted education, including links to provincial organizations, information about summer camps, and links to pages for kids.

Two other magazines that offer many practical home-learning ideas for parents are *Understanding Our Gifted* (published by Open Space Communications, see page 179) and *Gifted Education Press Quarterly* (get a lifetime subscription for a modest fee, see page 178).

In your quest to enrich your child's education and development, keep in mind that she needs downtime, too. She needs time each day to dawdle, to daydream, to savor as well as advance her learning. She needs exercise, play, and rest, too. What you're seeking is a mix of stimulation and relaxation, of curiosity and imagination, that will allow your child—and her multitude of gifts—to thrive. In making your home the haven where this can happen, you're setting the stage for success in school as well.

Take a Stand!

Start now to build a small home library of books, newsletters, magazines, videos, games, and other learning materials for you and your child. See pages 171–182 for ideas. Acquiring resources entails some expense, so plan to gather your library together gradually. If there are specific books or materials you know you'd like, put them on your birthday or holiday wish list!

Your home library will help you when you need specific guidance, are stumped for ideas, aren't sure you understand a specific term or school policy, or want to back up your advocacy efforts with research. It can offer your child a place to store and explore his favorite books and magazines. Add a comfortable chair or some floor pillows, and it will become a welcoming reading corner.

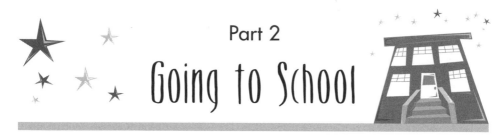

Part 2
Going to School

Gifted students need and deserve an education that provides many things: Learning experiences that develop mastery and knowledge along with challenges to critical and creative thinking. Opportunities to apply and experiment with what they learn. Exposure to a wide variety of subjects and projects to develop the full range of their intellectual, creative, and artistic gifts. Experiences with other gifted children. Teachers trained in the special needs of gifted kids.

Some schools offer many of these opportunities. Others offer a few, and some, none. How does your school measure up? How does it identify giftedness in children? What programs does it offer? What can you do to support and improve what your school is doing for your child?

Maybe your gifted son is about to enter kindergarten and you're wondering what the school will be able to offer him. Maybe you've been asked permission to have your daughter tested for the gifted education program, and you're not even sure what the program is. Maybe your child's school year is coming to an end and you have only a general idea about the gifted education services available for students in higher grades. Maybe you're looking to change schools or have recently moved to a new community. Maybe your child's gifted program isn't challenging enough. Or maybe your child isn't eligible for the gifted program, or has been dropped from it, and you don't understand why. Maybe your school has no special services for gifted kids.

To begin improving your child's school experience, you must learn what's available to you. You need to:

- Know your state guidelines.

- Know your district's and school's philosophy and/or mandate on gifted education.

- Learn how kids are selected for gifted services and what programs are available.

- Form a strong working relationship with your child's teacher or teachers.

- Get to know the other school staff—their roles and how they can help you and your child.

An effective advocate is an informed advocate. The more you understand, the more information you gather, the more empowered you will be to act on your child's behalf. Part 2 will guide you as you investigate and communicate with the school.

Chapter 6
Advocacy Is . . .
Understanding Gifted Education

My daughter Sheila has always been a good student. It never occurred to me that she could do more than just "good work" until she went to a special summer program for bright fifth and sixth graders. Frankly, I didn't even think she'd get into the program because her test scores aren't that high. When she takes tests she just freezes up and can't think. But this program accepts kids if they do well by other measures, such as parent input and samples of children's projects from home. I was amazed at the advanced work Sheila did that summer. By September she had a box full of inventions and original games she'd developed at camp. I began to see that her school hasn't been bringing out her true abilities. Her teacher for the summer program said Sheila learns best by doing, not by sitting and listening. When I showed Sheila's fifth-grade teacher and the district supervisor some of what Sheila did at the summer program, they offered to test her again for the accelerated class. But I don't think Sheila needs acceleration, if that just means moving faster through material she already finds boring. Sheila's talents come out in projects where she can experiment and create.

My bright, imaginative son disliked school and was labeled an "underachiever" by his teacher. Aaron's test scores disqualified him for the gifted program, and he was getting poor grades on assignments. When we talked with his teacher about the sophisticated computer programming Aaron does with his dad at home, she decided to refer Aaron to the school psychologist to see if he had a learning disability. Luckily for us, the psychologist knows a lot about gifted kids. She could see beyond Aaron's test scores and spotty school performance to his unique abilities. After talking with us and giving Aaron a series of individual intelligence and creativity tests, she recommended him for the gifted program.

An ideal system of identification and programming for gifted children would evaluate a child's school performance throughout the year, incorporating input from parents and teachers and using as many different sources of information as possible. Kids would have access to gifted programming as soon as their talents became apparent. The programming they received would fit their individual ways of being gifted. Such an open-ended approach, however, is rare in schools. According to the National Association for Gifted Children, of the approximately three million U.S. children considered gifted, only a little over half are reported to be receiving education appropriate to their needs. Why? For one thing, it requires more staff training and funding than most schools are able or willing to devote to gifted services. Another reason is that the importance schools place on meeting the needs of gifted kids and the ways giftedness is defined and funded can vary state by state, district by district—even school by school. Despite the fact that the U.S. has a national standard for identifying and educating gifted kids, that hasn't translated into specific policies and guidelines for meeting them.

This is markedly different from the situation for children with learning differences and disabilities. Unlike these children, gifted kids have very few legal rights, particularly in times when schools struggle to fund a variety of programs and are being required to do more and more standardized teaching so that children can pass grade-level tests. This lack of a national policy also contributes to the widespread myth that gifted kids don't need special support—that they'll succeed on their own.

Since the right of gifted children to an appropriate education is not guaranteed under any federal law, responsibility rests with the states. About 30 states have a mandate to serve gifted children; the others have legislation permitting, but not requiring, gifted education. And some of those mandates have no "teeth"—no provisions have been made for evaluating programs or for holding districts accountable. Most important, some states that require gifted education don't provide the money required to implement it.

Still, there are some hopeful signs for gifted kids and their parents. Educators are becoming more aware of the need to provide an education that's appropriate for high-ability students. Parent advocates are playing an important role in making this happen. Before you explore what your particular school has to offer, it helps to have a larger context and framework. What tools and practices are currently available and being used to identify gifted children? What types of programming exist? Becoming familiar with current practices in gifted education gives you the language and understanding to explore your child's situation knowledgeably.

HOW ARE GIFTED CHILDREN IDENTIFIED?

If a school has any kind of program for gifted students, it also must have ways of identifying such students. The purpose of identification is to find learners whose educational needs aren't being met by the core curriculum and to evaluate these children's needs in order to provide them with a program of learning that's appropriate for their specific talents and abilities. There are a number of tools available to help schools do this:

- standardized intelligence and achievement tests

- teacher recommendations based on grades and classroom observation

- creativity tests

- parent input

- portfolios

- interviews

- anecdotal information

Schools tend to weight these identification criteria in one of two ways. For the majority of schools, standardized test scores and teacher recommendations are considered most important; grades and class performance may also be taken into account. In other schools, a variety of criteria have equal weight in the evaluation process, allowing children with high ratings in at least one or two measures of ability to participate in the gifted program. This second, broader approach to identification is relatively uncommon in schools today. However, in some states—California, Texas, and Oregon, for example—schools are beginning to give more weight to measures other than standardized tests. This is true for some individual school districts in other states, too. A child whose scores aren't high enough on a standardized test—maybe because she freezes up in testing situations or has difficulty with the narrow, linear nature of the test items—may still qualify for a gifted program through alternative identification methods.

Standardized Tests

Standardized tests are norm-referenced, meaning that they've been developed and carefully monitored for validity with students of a particular grade, age, region of the country, gender, or some other characteristic. Ideally, a child's score reflects how he compares to other students like him in various ways at the national, state, or local level.

The most widely used standardized tests are group intelligence tests and group achievement tests. Individual intelligence tests may also be administered.

Group intelligence tests. These are popular because they're affordable and relatively easy to administer and score. Schools may give group intelligence tests to all students periodically as part of a regular standardized testing program. The scores for these tests are computed based on a child's grade level, not on the child's age, so while a score from a group test may look like an IQ, it is really much less precise. Group intelligence tests also have a *ceiling of difficulty*—a top level of performance the test can assess. For example, a group intelligence test for third graders may have a ceiling of seventh grade. This means that group tests aren't likely to identify highly gifted kids—those whose abilities are above a seventh-grade level. Though routinely used to identify students for gifted programs, most group intelligence tests aren't designed to do this. They are meant to tell teachers and parents how a child's ability compares with what he's achieving in school—not what his gifts and talents are.

Group achievement tests. In conjunction with other assessment information, group achievement tests are sometimes used to identify gifted students, even though, again, this isn't their intended purpose. They measure what students have learned or have been taught. Because the test items focus on the expected achievement of average students, standardized achievement tests don't do a good job of distinguishing individual differences among the most (and least) able students. Achievement tests often report grade-equivalent scores, which can be misleading. For example, a fifth grader may have a reading grade-equivalent score of 11.5. This does not mean that the child can read eleventh-grade material, but rather that his reading level is typical of the average eleventh grader. At best, standardized achievement tests identify children who may have learned more in school than those who score below them.

Schools that rely on standardized test scores to identify giftedness will probably miss some qualified students. Virtually all standardized tests have some bias toward the majority culture—the white middle class. This means that kids from other backgrounds are often at a disadvantage: the tests may not do a good job of measuring their skills and abilities.

As an example, consider a child whose first language isn't English. In school this child is probably identified as an ELL (English language learner) or an ESL (English as a second language) or LEP (limited English proficiency) learner. For this student, any test is in part a test of the child's facility with the English language. Since standardized tests aren't intended to test fluency in English, the child's score will be invalid in some ways and must be interpreted very carefully.

In addition, some kids do not test well. A child may be tired, anxious, ill, or preoccupied on the day of the test. A gifted child may have an extraordinarily high aptitude in abstract reasoning, but get average scores on achievement tests that focus on specific subject-area knowledge and skills. Some students—particularly creatively gifted kids—spend too much time mulling over test items. It's hard for them to restrict themselves to one answer, so they run out of time and get unreliably low scores.

Individual intelligence tests. Most individual intelligence tests are given by a trained psychologist. In general, individual intelligence tests compute scores based on a child's age, not grade. The ceiling of difficulty is likely to be higher than that on a group test. Results of an individual IQ test are typically divided into three areas: a full-scale score, also known as an IQ score; scores on two sub-scales, performance and verbal; and ten sub-test scores, which give clues to a child's strengths and weaknesses in specific areas. In many schools, the full-scale score must be 130 or greater in order for children to be included in gifted programs. Gifted education specialists agree that individual intelligence tests are more accurate than group tests in assessing intelligence—at least, intelligence as the majority culture defines it.

Given that many schools screen children for gifted programs based on school-wide tests administered once annually (usually in the spring), most gifted kids have one chance a year to be identified for gifted programming. Schools don't usually test a child again unless a learning problem is suspected.

Standardized Testing: Find Out **More**

For a truly comprehensive look at testing, contact the following resource:

ERIC/AE Test Locator
ERIC Clearinghouse on Assessment and Evaluation
1131 Shriver Laboratory, Building 075
University of Maryland
College Park, MD 20742
1-800-464-3742
www.ericae.net/testcol.htm
The Test Locator is a joint project of the ERIC Clearinghouse on Assessment and Evaluation, the Library and Reference Services Division of the Educational Testing Service, the Buros Institute of Mental Measurements at the University of Nebraska in Lincoln, the Region III Comprehensive Center at GW University, and Pro-Ed test publishers. Its database has descriptions of over 10,000 tests and research instruments. Included at the Web site is the Test Review Locator, which enables you to search for reviews of educational and psychological tests.

Frequently, individual testing is requested by a parent. When parents call me about having their child tested in this way, I often recommend that they go to a psychologist who tests gifted children *outside* the school. This is not to suggest that the school psychologist can't do the job. But psychologists in private practice with a focus on gifted kids tend to have more specialized knowledge about appropriate tests and testing environments.

> Our fifth grader, Timothy, has some trouble with reading, but he absolutely loves history. We knew he was bright, but the school and teacher didn't seem to agree. So we finally decided to have him tested by an independent psychologist. We learned that Tim has an unusually good memory, a sophisticated vocabulary, creative talent—and dyslexia. With that information, we met with the school curriculum coordinator. We had to negotiate a few things, but the end result was that we got some early release time for Tim so he could work with a college student who shares his passion for history. The school incorporated special reading instruction with a tutor into his school day. This system has worked well, and Tim's now showing real enthusiasm for school.

Sometimes the school or a state or local gifted organization can recommend private practitioners who specialize in testing for high ability. Otherwise, parents can check out non-school-based options such as centers for talent development, specialized learning centers, and programs in colleges and universities. Private testing can be expensive. Sometimes universities and clinical psychologists are willing to make special payment arrangements for families with limited incomes. Don't hesitate to ask about the possibility of a sliding-fee or extended-payment plan.

Teacher Recommendations

Along with test scores, teacher recommendations are the most widely used criteria for identifying gifted children. Teachers usually nominate their students based on test scores, grades, class performance, and such behaviors as attentiveness, persistence to task, motivation, and participation. The more a teacher knows about the characteristics of giftedness and how they may show themselves, the more accurate that teacher's recommendations will be. So much depends on the particular teacher! If he takes into account the whole child—things like learning styles, imaginative thinking, and intense sensitivities as well as grades and class performance—he's more likely to recommend children who could be overlooked by test scores and grades alone. On the other hand, a teacher who places high value on such qualities as neatness, ability to follow instructions, and good behavior may miss gifted kids who are highly imaginative, independent, messy, or uncooperative. Kids whose behavior has become a problem—often because they're bored and unchallenged—may also be overlooked.

Teachers often use checklists when they nominate a child for gifted programs. Most checklists have a section where various behaviors are listed under specific categories (such as academic achievement or creative expression). Some schools offer very detailed checklists. For example, under a category called "analytical ability" might be specific abilities like "understands cause and effect in mathematical operations" and "can compare two processes and note significant differences." The advantage of checklists is that they can include abilities and talents that tests can't measure.

Other Criteria

What other methods can schools use to identify gifted children? There are several, often referred to collectively as *multiple criteria*. Because many of these approaches can include input from parents, they have the potential to be critical tools for your advocacy:

Creativity tests. Creativity tests have been around for a while but are still not widely used to identify giftedness. These kind of tests are fun for kids and show promise as a way of identifying creatively gifted students. Many of the published creativity tests were influenced by E. Paul Torrance's research on fluency, flexibility, originality, and elaboration (described, along with additional readings on the subject, in "Creativity and Giftedness: Find Out More," page 11). Torrance's *Tests of Creative Thinking* include these four aspects. In another of Torrance's tests, *Thinking Creatively in Action and Movement,* the examiner must participate in the activities with the child. A handful of other tests that measure creativity include:

- *The Creativity Tests for Children* (CTC) developed by J.P. Guilford et al includes measures of semantics, visual/figural processing, and divergent thinking abilities.

- *The Group Inventory for Finding Talent* (GIFT) created by Sylvia Rimm measures creativity as defined by independence, curiosity, perseverance, flexibility, and breadth of thinking. This instrument takes the form of a student self-report.

- Joe Khatena and E. Paul Torrance's *Khatena-Torrance Creative Perception Inventory* (KTCPI) measures aspects of authority, self-confidence, inquisitiveness, awareness of others, environmental sensitivity, intuitiveness, self-strength, intellectuality, individuality, and artistry. Two self-tests are combined in this inventory: What Kind of a Person Are You? (WKOPAY) and Something About Myself (SAM).

- The *Screening Assessment for Gifted Elementary Students* (SAGES) by Susan Johnson and Ann Corn, one of the more commonly used instruments for identifying giftedness, includes a component to assess creativity.

Parent input. When parent recommendations are directly sought, the requests frequently come in the form of a letter from the school with a checklist of characteristics and space for comments. If your child's school actively seeks input from parents when identifying gifted children, you are fortunate; the norm is for schools *not* to invite parent input for decisions about who will receive gifted services. For schools that have gifted programs for primary students (those in prekindergarten or kindergarten through second grade), it's a little more common to solicit and use input from parents. In any case, parents have the right to volunteer information about their child. The most practical thing a parent can do is arrange a meeting with the gifted education coordinator or teacher and bring notes and observations along with examples of projects and other work the child has done at home.

Portfolio assessment. With portfolio assessment, children are evaluated based on samples of what they've done or produced in school: writing, art, science experiments, mathematical problem solving, inventions, and so forth. A teacher or classroom paraprofessional (trained teacher's aide) usually puts together the portfolio, sometimes with help from parents who can add examples from a home portfolio. Portfolio assessment gives kids the opportunity to show their best work—often work they've produced over time in unpressured, open environments. Three things make this kind of assessment useful for placing gifted students in appropriate programs:

- Children frequently reveal exceptional abilities and talents that may be hidden or go unrecognized in a traditional curriculum.

- Children can demonstrate ability not identified on a standardized test.

- When standardized testing has identified a child for gifted programming, a portfolio can give a clearer and more complex picture of a child's gifts.

Interviews. Though used for gifted identification only rarely, an interview with a child can provide valuable information about the child's interests, talents, learning styles, preferred intelligences, and sensitivities. Interviews can also resolve any concerns teachers, administrators, or parents may have about a child's participation in the gifted program.

How this type of interview is conducted varies from district to district. In most cases, the interviewer is a gifted education coordinator or gifted teacher who meets with the child privately, without the parent. When conducted responsibly, an interview is informal, like a conversation. The child doesn't feel put on the spot or fearful that the adult asking questions is testing her for the right answers. It also helps if the child is asked to bring in some project or work sample. Kids talk about themselves more easily when they can focus on something they've worked on or enjoyed doing. As long as everyone realizes that it's very difficult for a child to sit across a table from an adult and speak freely, interviews can yield interesting and revealing insights about a child's particular gifts.

Anecdotal information. Examples and stories describing evidence that a child is gifted can come from a teacher, a parent, or anyone else who knows or has worked with that child. Anecdotes are different from information noted on checklists, because the adult tells or writes about real examples from a child's life—what the circumstances were, what the child said or did, and how the example demonstrates unique ability. Keeping a notebook will serve a parent well in providing anecdotes about a child's gifts. Parents can share the anecdotes at a conference with the teacher or provide them in writing to the teacher, gifted education coordinator, psychologist, or other personnel evaluating the child.

Identification: Find Out More

California Association for the Gifted (CAG)
5777 West Century Boulevard, Suite 1670
Los Angeles, CA 90045
310-215-1898
www.cagifted.org
The spring 2000 (vol. 21, no. 2) issue of CAG's national magazine, *Communicator,* is devoted to the subject of identification. It explores a variety of concerns including common problems in identification, finding gifted English learners, nontraditional screening, what parents can expect, when a child doesn't qualify, and the roles and responsibilities of educators and parents.

Contexts for Promise: Noteworthy Practices and Innovations in the Identification of Gifted Students by Carolyn Callahan, Carol A. Tomlinson, and Paula M. Pizzat (Storrs, CT: National Research Center on the Gifted and Talented, 1994). A collection of case studies summarizing the results of research at five universities, this book presents information on identification and programming for a variety of underserved populations of gifted children including economically disadvantaged children, twice exceptional learners, and those from minority cultures.

Identification procedures should reflect the kind of program offered. If a gifted program is heavily oriented toward math and science, then tests and recommendations should reveal children's performance in those areas. If a program emphasizes creativity and hands-on activities, academic achievement tests shouldn't be the major identification method.

What About Your Child?

The way your school identifies gifted students can tell you a lot about the school's attitudes and priorities:

- Has your child been through an identification process? If so, was she identified by her school as gifted? Are you comfortable with the process that identified her?

- If your child didn't qualify for a gifted program, what criteria were used? Standardized tests? Teacher observations and recommendations? Were you asked for input? What other methods of evaluating your child's ability would fit her better?

- If your child hasn't been through a process of identification, what do you think would be the best ways for the school to evaluate her for a gifted program?

WHAT EDUCATIONAL PROGRAMS EXIST FOR GIFTED STUDENTS?

Many kids have exceptional ability in some areas but not in others, and schools with the most effective services for gifted learners recognize that many kids are gifted in certain specific ways, not necessarily in all areas of the curriculum. If children in a gifted program are required to do advanced work in all subjects, some will probably struggle.

Broadly, gifted programs are developed using three strategies:

- acceleration
- enrichment
- differentiation

Acceleration

Acceleration doesn't mean simply doing what everyone else does, only faster. Gifted kids need the opportunity to move quickly through material they already know—or to skip material entirely, if they can show they've mastered it. Many also do best when they're allowed to progress through school based not on their age but on their abilities and what they already know—and when there's no ceiling that places limits on their learning. For example, if a child is ready for algebra in fifth grade, an ideal system must not only permit this but support it, even though most elementary schools don't offer algebra as part of their standard curriculum.

Three typical ways to accelerate gifted students' progress through school are early entrance, grade skipping, and continuous progress.

Early entrance. With early entrance, children begin kindergarten before the usual starting age or date. Usually done on a school psychologist's recommendation based on pretesting and interviewing, this option allows kids with sufficient maturity to be challenged, rather than bored, by kindergarten. Though gifted education specialists recognize early entrance as an appropriate choice for some young gifted children, the great majority of schools don't often recommend or support it. Still, parents can and should ask the school to consider this option if they feel their child would benefit.

Grade skipping. Grade skipping involves advancing kids through grades ahead of the usual age or date or allowing double promotions so they skip a grade level altogether. Sometimes, too, a gifted child may skip a grade or more in a particular subject, like science or math.

There are drawbacks to both early entrance and grade skipping—some kids may not be emotionally mature enough to handle this option, while others don't like being separated from their classmates. However, in many cases a gifted child's true peers are his intellectual peers, rather than children his own age. Some gifted kids thrive when they're accelerated in this way.

Continuous progress. With this method, students advance through the curriculum according to ability rather than grade level. Also called *mastery learning,* this option allows students to move through material at their own pace. They usually take a pretest for each new concept or skill and, if they demonstrate mastery, move on to more advanced work. Most commonly offered for subjects taught sequentially, such as math, continuous progress allows gifted children to avoid what they complain about most: having to repeat material they already know. However, continuous progress may not be the answer for a creative child who craves enrichment and independent work.

Enrichment

Options that provide enrichment replace or extend the regular curriculum with programs that focus on higher-level skills such as analytical thinking and problem solving. Kids might take field trips, do special projects, or work with professionals (writers or scientists, for example) in areas related to the curriculum. Sound enrichment programs and classes do more than just interest and entertain a gifted student: they engage the child's abilities with a focus on critical and creative thinking and activities that provide the chance to explore a subject in depth.

Pull-out programs. These are part-time programs in which kids leave their regular classroom to attend classes with other gifted and talented students, taught by specially trained resource teachers. The amount of instructional time spent in pull-out gifted classes varies from district to district. It can be as little as one hour a week or as much as one full day a week (though this is rare).

The main advantage of pull-out programs is that gifted students get to work with their intellectual peers. However, for most gifted kids these programs offer only a part-time solution to a full-time condition. Gifted students are gifted all the time—not just when they're in a pull-out class. Also, pull-out programs can be disruptive, causing kids to miss special events or information in their regular classrooms. If pull-out programs are done well, teachers work together to coordinate tests, homework, special events, and the introduction of important topics in the regular classroom so gifted kids don't miss out or feel burdened by extra work.

Creative arts. Not all schools offer creative arts as a service for gifted students, but enrichment in art, music, and drama presents distinct opportunities for developing creativity and enhancing advanced skills like divergent thinking. Many schools with arts programming offer drawing, painting, and music; others offer drama—usually plays or skits directed by regular classroom teachers. Parents of creatively gifted students should evaluate the school's arts program. They may be able to negotiate an arrangement whereby, for example, their child is allowed to work in the art room when the class is reviewing material she already knows, or whenever she has completed her academic work or tested out of particular content.

Supplemental programs. Supplemental programs take place outside the regular school day, usually during the summer and on weekends. These may be sponsored by the school or district. They may also be offered through a university or organized by parents and teachers. Classes often include a wide range of subjects, exploring topics rarely or never covered in school. They emphasize critical and creative thinking, application, invention, hands-on learning, and independent projects. Since these experiences are usually ungraded, students tend to take greater risks with their ideas. They often have the opportunity to develop a new interest or discover a talent. Like in-school programs, good supplemental programs are carefully constructed and have clearly stated objectives. The programs usually encourage parent involvement and may even offer parent workshops and seminars.

Mentorships. A mentorship links a student with a teacher, a community person, a parent, or an older student who acts as a friend, guide, and coach. Mentorships are especially valuable for gifted kids with an intense interest in a particular subject, such as architecture, musical composition, science, art, computers, zoology, or journalism. Usually, the child's classroom teacher or a gifted education coordinator keeps track of progress through a learning contract or an agreement set up by the teacher, mentor, and student. A fourth grader working with a seventh-grade science teacher, a child working individually with the art teacher one afternoon a week, a student given permission to stay home one morning a week to work with a parent—each is participating in a different form of mentorship.

Distance learning. With distance learning, a teacher can teach students in more than one school simultaneously. Typically, students participating in distance learning work via computer or watch a teacher on closed-circuit TV. Some districts also use interactive videoconferencing so students can participate directly. Distance learning is often used in rural areas to widen gifted kids' opportunities for enrichment and advanced instruction.

Differentiation

Differentiation is the process of adapting the regular classroom curriculum to meet each student's individual needs. Though not all classroom teachers are trained to use differentiation, many sensitive teachers do it naturally. The ideal is to differentiate instruction for all students, but some teachers do so mainly for gifted children and children with LD (learning differences). It's valuable to understand how differentiation works, because it offers opportunities for challenging gifted learners even in schools with little or no gifted programming.

The simplest explanation of curriculum differentiation is that it varies content, process, and product. What does this mean?

- To differentiate *content*, a teacher gives students different material to learn within the curriculum. For example, if the lesson plan calls for students to read *Across Five Aprils*, a gifted student who has already read the book could read *The Red Badge of Courage* instead.

- To differentiate *process*, the teacher might allow some learners to work through more quickly (and some more slowly) than others or to investigate more deeply.

- To differentiate *product*, students would use varying ways to show what they'd learned. If the class is completing a unit on the American Civil War, some students might work in teams to prepare summarizing reports while others create maps charting the war's strategic battles or write analysis of the causes of the war and the conditions that came in its wake.

Teachers typically differentiate all three of these main curricular elements with children of varying abilities and learning needs. Gifted students need the regular curriculum modified or adapted to their special strengths. They need adjustments in the way material is presented, how it is paced, and its level of difficulty. For your gifted child—whether the differentiated assignment relates to content, process, or product—you'll want to look for these components:

- *acceleration*—providing gifted students the opportunity to move quickly to more advanced material

- *complexity*—challenging kids to explore relationships between events or phenomena, to look at an issue from different points of view, or to use different approaches to solve a problem

- *novelty*—introducing a child to an area of study that is new to him, often by means of an independent project devised by the student and teacher together

- *depth*—digging deeper into a subject in order to learn more than the regular curriculum offers (for example, by examining patterns, researching the roots of a problem or situation, or analyzing the ethics of an issue)

With these elements in mind, here are some ways teachers can differentiate instruction for gifted learners:

Curriculum compacting. This strategy involves compressing material into a shorter time frame by allowing a child to demonstrate mastery of content he already knows, often through pretests. The student then moves on to more advanced material or works with his teacher to devise individual projects. Kids may either skip parts of the curriculum or move quickly through early lessons. For example, a student who has mastered computation might finish the whole year's computation lessons in a few months and then move on to more advanced math, such as the laws of exponents, the lore of prime numbers, or other topics from number theory.

This practice has become a viable option for gifted students in the regular classroom. A teacher can recommend the process, or the gifted education coordinator or a parent may request that the curriculum be compacted. The teacher and coordinator, or teacher and parent, decide how the child will show that he's mastered material, which learning will be compressed or eliminated, and what advanced work will be added to the child's program. The teacher and student often create a learning contract or set of agreements so the student knows what's expected of him and the teacher can manage the arrangement.

Ability grouping. This method puts students with similar skills together for instruction in a particular subject area, often math or reading. The group might meet in the regular classroom or in the classroom of a specially trained teacher. Grouping gifted students by ability allows them to learn together but avoids permanent grouping arrangements (known as *tracking*) for students of other ability levels. A typical use of ability grouping is in reading groups. A gifted child in the fast reading group would probably stay there throughout the year. Other students, however, would change groups as their reading skills improved.

Flexible grouping. This method groups students based on interests and/or abilities on an assignment-by-assignment basis. Like most educational strategies, the success of flexible grouping depends a great deal on the teacher. A teacher who individualizes instruction for all kids will have an easier time using this option than a teacher who prefers whole-group instruction. One way teachers can offer challenge is by giving gifted students the opportunity to work and interact with their intellectual peers.

Flexible groups are usually dissolved when the instructional goal is reached or the project completed. A group may form again later in the year with different members. For example, for a particular project or unit, the teacher may group gifted kids with other highly motivated students interested in the topic. Or the teacher may give different assignments to each small group, placing gifted kids together and assigning them an especially challenging topic. Sometimes called *tiered assignments,* this strategy also enables the teacher to target the learning needs of each group of students without causing them to feel they're being placed in an ability group (since each group is doing a different assignment).

Cluster grouping. This method groups students of the same grade level who have been identified as gifted and places them together in the same class. In some schools, five to eight gifted students, usually those in the top five percent of ability in a particular grade, are grouped in the classroom of a teacher who has training in teaching gifted kids. The other students in that class are of mixed ability. This arrangement is valuable for several reasons. When a teacher is working with several gifted students rather than one or two, taking the time to differentiate curriculum for them can be more manageable—particularly when a teacher has a special interest in gifted education. Perhaps most important, gifted kids profit from learning with others like them.

Don't confuse cluster grouping with cooperative learning. Cooperative learning typically organizes students in mixed-ability groups. For gifted kids, this means they often end up doing most of the work or helping others. While this might be fine if done occasionally, it's not always in gifted children's best interests. Cluster groups give kids the challenge and stimulation of working with others of similar high ability.

Another grouping possibility is to cluster gifted students during times when material is being reviewed. Gifted kids who don't need the review might be grouped together to work on activities or projects that present extra challenge and enrichment. These alternative assignments might be done in the library, resource room, or classroom learning center, where the kids won't distract the rest of the class.

Interdisciplinary curriculum. Teachers can also differentiate instruction by integrating various subject areas to expand the study of a basic theme or unit. A unit on ocean life, for example, could draw on science, art, history, geography, and mathematics to show the complexity of the subject. This kind of integration allows students to develop a deeper understanding of a topic, giving them the flexibility to explore a theme from multiple points of view. You may find an interdisciplinary approach used in pull-out programs, in the regular classroom, and in assignments for cluster groups.

Self-contained classrooms. Full-time classrooms for gifted students are found far less frequently than the various part-time options, but they offer many advantages, particularly in the primary grades. In a self-contained gifted classroom, thinking skills can be taught in the context of the various content areas. Long-term projects are more feasible, individualization and acceleration are easier to implement, and teachers and students have time to develop closer working relationships. A special full-time classroom, however, doesn't guarantee a quality gifted education program unless the learning environment is structured appropriately, the curriculum is well designed, and the teachers are adequately prepared.

Individualization. For gifted kids, individualized instruction usually involves independent study projects that students help select. Kids are encouraged to pursue their special interests and develop their talents, regardless of whether these relate to the school's regular curriculum. Kids work at their own pace on projects that fit their special abilities, interests, and learning needs. Teachers usually monitor independent work and devise a system with students that outlines specific activities as well as learning goals.

Sometimes, teachers ease kids into independent work. For example, the teacher may first offer a child a few specific choices of topics, devising a learning contract with precise goals and a timeline so the student knows exactly what's expected. Later, the child and teacher may come up with topics, goals, and timelines together. Eventually, the child chooses topics himself, creates his own goals and objectives (approved by the teacher), and completes the project according to his own time table—which may be renegotiated if he finds new lines of inquiry. Children who do independent projects should have the opportunity to share the results or products with classmates, not just with the teacher.

What About Your Child?

Think about what you know about your child's abilities, talents, strengths, preferred intelligences, and personality. Ask yourself:

- Is my child getting an education that fully supports his particular gifts?

- What is my child's school doing to meet my child's educational needs? What else could be done?

- What kinds of programs would be most appropriate and effective for my child?

Take a Stand!

Find out where your state stands on the issue of gifted education. It's important to learn both the laws governing your state and the realities your particular school or district faces in regard to funding. Starting from here, you'll have a clearer picture of what's possible in terms of helping your child as well as what, realistically, the school will be able and willing to offer.

Probably the easiest way to get state-level information is to contact your state's gifted association. You can write or phone the National Association for Gifted Children or visit its Web site, which provides information and links to state organizations. (You'll find information about NAGC on page 62. You'll also find the Gifted Canada site on page 63, which has links to provincial organizations.) Tape the literature or computer printout that highlights state standards in your notebook for future reference.

Joining your state association is always a good idea. In addition to having a source for advice and information on your state's policies, you can also receive the association's publications and attend conferences where you can learn more about gifted issues.

Chapter 7
Advocacy Is . . .
Getting to Know Your Child's School

I walked into the principal's office yesterday to talk about my child. Mr. Gonzalez was a really nice, down-to-earth, relaxed sort of guy—not at all like the principal I had when I was a kid. But I was still feeling the same way I did 30 years ago when I got sent to the principal's office!

As I talked with the media specialist one morning, I discovered that the library offered a fiction-writing workshop twice a week for the ninth graders, led by a published author. My daughter, Shannon, is in seventh grade, but she's a gifted writer. I was excited about this special program and wondered if I could get Shannon into it. I asked Shannon's English teacher if Shannon could, on a trial basis, leave class for the workshops. He agreed, as long as Shannon kept up with her regular classwork. She did, gladly. Those workshops were wonderful for Shannon! She has always loved writing but has never had the opportunity to work with other people who like to write as much as she does—especially with a professional writer. If I hadn't been chatting with the media specialist, I may never have heard about this program.

You've begun to learn about gifted education and have thought about the kind of support your child needs to develop her unique abilities and talents. It's now time to get familiar with your child's school—how it defines and identifies gifted children, what it does to meet their educational needs, who's responsible for carrying out the programming for gifted kids, and what this means for your child.

Many parents feel some anxiety about approaching teachers or administrators to ask for information, make requests for their child, or express concerns about the curriculum. Memories of your own school experiences may get in the way. Even if the memories are good ones, it's easy to feel a little intimidated.

For many parents, a big concern is that they'll be considered "pushy." You might need to remind yourself often that it's *not* pushy to seek out information, get involved, and support your child so she can thrive in school. You can be respectful yet persistent. You can empathize with the pressures the teacher is under and still assert your right—and responsibility—to advocate for your child. If you don't do this, who will? Think of what you're doing as exploring, learning, gathering information, and making connections. Think of yourself as a collaborator with the school in getting your child's needs met. It might help to write this note to yourself and read it every day: "My child deserves an appropriate education. My job is to work with the school to see that she gets it."

If you want a little moral support, enlist a partner, friend, or relative to go with you to school to meet or talk with the teacher, get to know the other school personnel, and learn about what programs and practices are in place for gifted children. Think of this person as *your* advocate.

WHAT'S THE POLICY?

With information about your state's guidelines for gifted education in mind, your first step at school is to find out the guidelines that your school follows in identifying and creating learning programs for gifted children. Schools with established services for gifted students usually have clear guidelines for their programs. Guidelines generally include a specific definition of giftedness, criteria for identifying gifted students, descriptions of the services offered, and goals for the program. For public schools, call the school your child attends or the district office and request a copy of the policy and guidelines. If your child attends a private school, ask the principal or dean for the school's policy statement.

Read the guidelines carefully, noting your questions and aspects of the policy that have special importance for your child. Compare your school's or district's policy with your state's guidelines; see if your school is doing what your state's and district's philosophy statements call for. Place the guidelines in your notebook so you can refer to them readily.

Who Will Answer Your Questions?

You'll want to talk with people who can fill in any gaps in your understanding. The best people to answer your questions about the school's gifted program are those who staff it. Staff members who can answer your questions about gifted programming may include:

- **Gifted education coordinator.** Usually hired by the district, this person coordinates programs, initiates services if they're not already in place, supervises teachers of gifted students, and evaluates programs and services. If you have a gifted education coordinator, he or she can explain the philosophy and goals of gifted education in your district. This person probably also has a good grasp of gifted education in general—what it aims to accomplish, for whom, and how. Usually, the gifted education coordinator travels from school to school; in rare cases, a coordinator is assigned to one school.

- **Trained G/T (gifted and talented) resource teachers.** In the most successful programs, teachers are either certified in gifted and talented education or have extensive background in teaching gifted students. Special programming for gifted students (such as pull-out programs) is usually handled either by the gifted education coordinator or a resource teacher.

- **Director of special education.** Some schools assign responsibility for gifted programs and services to the director of special education. This person is concerned with *all* special education programs and services—for children with learning differences, disabilities, and behavior concerns as well as gifted kids. Depending on workload, training, and time constraints, she or he may not be as knowledgeable as a gifted education coordinator about gifted children or aware of everything going on in the gifted program.

- **Curriculum coordinator.** If your school or district has no gifted education coordinator or trained resource teachers, and if the director of special education has little or no responsibility for gifted students, you could approach the curriculum coordinator. This person can explain the school's curriculum goals and may be sympathetic to your gifted child's learning needs.

- **School psychologist.** If your child isn't doing well in the regular classroom even though test scores or out-of-school performance demonstrate high ability, you may want someone to test and evaluate your child individually. The school psychologist can be a helpful advocate in this situation. School psychologists sometimes assist in resolving problems with gifted children who need a different placement.

If your school hasn't designated anyone specifically to administer gifted services, talk with the principal, dean, or headmaster.

How Does the School Define and Identify Giftedness?
The school's gifted education policy guidelines should spell out how giftedness is defined and how gifted children are identified. Some school's definitions of giftedness are comprehensive and inclusive; others are restrictive. Most schools define gifted children as those kids who show high

academic ability, demonstrate advanced mastery of skills and content, and consistently perform above the norm in class and on standardized tests. These schools place less emphasis on students with exceptional creative or artistic talent (if they're not also academic achievers) and those who show their capabilities in nontraditional ways—such as a child who likes to improvise and experiment rather than follow an assignment to the letter.

What Programs and Services Does the School Provide?

The specifics of the school's gifted education program should also be explained in the policy statement. The schools best able to meet the needs of gifted children tend to combine in-class learning opportunities (differentiation, flexible grouping, and independent work) with other options (such as curriculum compacting, special projects, pull-out sessions with other gifted kids, and accelerated instruction).

How Does the School Evaluate Its Programs?

No matter what sort of program your school has implemented, evaluation should be part of the design. The school should regularly assess the effectiveness of all special services offered gifted students. Kids' academic progress, social growth, decision-making skills, and leadership abilities should be considered as indicators of the program's strengths or weaknesses. Weaknesses need to be addressed and a plan devised to address them. Strengths need to be analyzed so they can continue.

The most effective evaluation processes involve students, parents, and teachers. Students might be interviewed or asked to fill out a questionnaire about what they like most and least about the program, what they'd like to see changed, and how they think the program has helped them. Parents might be asked whether they want their children to continue in the program, what they'd like to see changed, and how their child has benefited. Teachers might fill out self-evaluation and program evaluation questionnaires. They should have regular staff meetings and regular opportunities to attend seminars and conferences and to visit other programs. This will help them both evaluate their own school's services more knowledgeably and discover additional ideas for supporting gifted learners.

If an evaluation of the program isn't clearly described in the policy statement, ask about it. You have the right to know how often your school's program is evaluated, in what ways, and with what results.

GET TO KNOW YOUR CHILD'S TEACHER

It's a wise strategy to meet with the teacher in a friendly, informal way *before* you begin advocating for your gifted child. Parents who have had positive encounters with their child's teacher have a much better chance of gaining a sympathetic ear than those who approach teachers as near strangers. In an elementary school, this means getting to know the regular classroom teacher as well as the gifted resource teacher, if your school has one. At the middle-school level, there are often advisory groups meeting 20–30 minutes or more a day in which the teacher gets to know children individually. In this case, you'll want to start building a relationship with this advisory teacher and with at least some of the subject-area teachers as well.

An effective way to begin learning about teachers is by talking to your child. Ask questions like these:

- How do you like your teacher? How are the two of you getting along?

- Is the reading you do in class interesting? Do you get to try out your ideas? How?

- What are some of your school projects? What kinds of activities are you doing that you especially like?

- What do you like best about school? Why do you like it?

- What don't you like to do? Why don't you like it?

- If you could change anything about school this year, what would you change?

Ask questions in a conversational way. Don't grill your child or ask everything at once. This way you'll begin to get a feel for how comfortable your child is in his classroom and how he's getting along with the teacher— preliminary impressions before you meet the teacher in person.

Introduce yourself to the teacher as early in the school year as you can. You might do this at an open house or PTA meeting, or informally when you're dropping off or picking up your child. Do all you can to begin to develop your relationship in a positive, affirming way. Teachers hear lots of complaints and demands—from parents, from students, and from other school personnel. Like everyone else, they like to feel appreciated and valued. Share anything you can think of that your child has liked about the class. Present yourself as a supportive parent who recognizes the teacher's efforts to meet students' needs.

Offer to help in the classroom in some way that your schedule permits. You might volunteer to:

- do a special activity with the class

- chaperone a field trip

- act as a teacher's aide

- tutor kids or help guide individual projects

- help with class displays or performances

- assist with computer software

- type handouts or make phone calls

- find library books to use with special units of study

If you can't volunteer during the regular school day, your help is still important. There are plenty of tasks, like managing a phone-calling tree or helping with mailings, that you might do at home. You can still communicate with the teacher (by phone, note, or email) and build rapport. Helping out and communicating in whatever ways you can will give you some real insight into your child's learning environment. You'll also be showing the teacher you're interested in the whole class, not just in issues pertaining to your own child.

In your early, informal contacts with your child's teacher, try to find out how much she knows about teaching gifted kids. You can gain some sense of this by observing her teaching style while you're helping in the classroom and by listening carefully to comments she makes about your child and other high-ability students. Most general teacher certification programs don't require coursework in gifted education, so if she's attuned to the needs of gifted kids, it's probably because she went out of her way to learn more about it. That in itself says something about this teacher.

What Makes an Effective Teacher?

As you get to know your child's teacher, ask yourself:

- Does the teacher seem sensitive to students' individual abilities and learning preferences?

- Is she flexible and creative in her approach to the curriculum?

- Does she appear open to suggestions, both from parents and from other staff members?

- Does she individualize instruction as much as possible?

- Has she created a stimulating learning space with plenty of materials and resources for independent and small-group work?

- Is she aware of the typical characteristics of gifted kids and compassionate in response to their social and emotional needs?

Use time spent in the classroom to be helpful, get to know more about the class and the school, and begin building a bond with the teacher. Don't try to talk about your child's needs while you're at school to help in class. Schedule a conference to do this. (For more on this, see "Arrange a Conference with the Teacher," pages 103–113.)

When the teacher does something special for the class or provides some experience that your child loves, be quick to express your gratitude either in person or through a note.

Dear Mrs. Gaynor,

I knew Leah was in good hands when she came home and told me the science teacher had given her a special project to do on crystals and crystal patterns. I'd heard that the fifth grade was doing an interdisciplinary study of patterns, and I'd hoped this would mean Leah would get to really dig into something in both science and math. She is excited about her independent project and has already begun doing research at the library and on the Internet. Thanks so much for the care you have taken to support Leah's interests.

Nadia Rominaski

Visiting with the teacher, offering to help out, and expressing gratitude for her efforts may not guarantee cooperation when you advocate for your child, but it will surely strengthen your chances and reduce any anxieties you have about discussing problems and suggesting solutions.

GET TO KNOW THE REST OF THE SCHOOL

Don't stop with the teacher—introduce yourself and talk with other staff members as well. Getting to know school staff is as much about *creating* advocates as it is about being one. There are all sorts of people who could play a pivotal role in your child's learning opportunities. Introduce yourself to other teachers who work with your child and to the librarian or media specialist, the counselor or psychologist, the principal, the assistant principal, the curriculum coordinator, the gifted education specialist, and other parent volunteers as well.

Make the effort to get to know school staff before your child has a problem or you must schedule a conference. That way, when you meet to talk about your child's learning needs, you'll have a sense of the different personalities at work—their perspectives, biases, and philosophies of education.

What If You've Gotten Off to a Bad Start?

If you and the teacher or school have developed a relationship that's tense or even adversarial, you might be wondering how to salvage the situation. Maybe you feel the teacher hasn't been open to your well-meaning overtures. Maybe you wish you'd approached the teacher and school less stridently. Whatever the case, take steps to turn the situation around.

If you think you owe the teacher an apology, offer one. If you feel the teacher's been closed-minded or unfriendly, take the high road. Ask what you can do to get your relationship on firmer ground. You might say, "It seems we've gotten off to a rocky start, and I'd really like to change that. What can I do to support you and the students in your class? I'd like to help out in whatever way I can."

Take a look at the school's physical layout, too. Is the atmosphere friendly? Is children's work displayed? Check out your child's classroom. How is the room arranged? Are students engaged and relaxed, or do you sense tension? If you were a child, would you enjoy being in this classroom? What about the library or media center? Are there areas where children interested in specific themes or subjects can do research? Are computers available? How can children use them? Visit the art room. Do the projects look interesting? Are students experimenting with different media or using materials in unusual ways?

At some point, write down some of your impressions of the school in your notebook. Think about the insight you're gaining in terms of *your* child's abilities, talents, interests, and needs. Is this school an inviting place for your child? What might make it more so?

Look into activities and special programs offered after school and during the school day. See what might be especially suitable for your child. Because you'll be getting to know staff people, you may be able to negotiate your child's participation in activities that ordinarily don't include her grade level. Many schools offer art, music, and drama classes, as well as science, math, chess, and foreign language clubs. For some gifted children, especially in schools where resources are scarce, these opportunities can make an enormous difference in their experience at school.

DO A REALITY CHECK

You've investigated how your child's school identifies and serves gifted children. You've gotten to know the teacher and some other staff and familiarized yourself with what the school has to offer. Now it's time to pragmatically assess what you can expect from the school and how you might best approach your advocacy. It's essential that you do this reality check so you can proceed to support and shape your child's education in the most logical, effective way possible.

Maybe your child readily fits the school's definition of giftedness. Maybe the school has in place a thriving gifted education program that's well funded and fully supported by the administration and teachers. Maybe your child's teacher has been well trained in meeting the needs of gifted kids, and the two of you are in complete agreement on how to ensure a rich educational experience for your child. If so, you—and your child—are fortunate indeed.

The likelihood, though, is that the picture's not quite so rosy. You may find that your child doesn't fit the school's definition of giftedness. Or that the school's identification profile doesn't include his unique abilities. Or that the programs and services for gifted children are limited, with little to offer your child. You may even find that your child's school has no gifted programming at all.

What If Your Child Doesn't Qualify?

Our family emigrated from Uganda to England. We came to the U.S. last year, when my son was ten and my daughter eight. Because their school in England offered an advanced program, and because both my children are gifted, they're ahead of the students here in their knowledge and skills. However, they've been placed in the ESL program because they're Ugandan and have accents. The school doesn't allow children to participate in the gifted program until they're out of ESL. My children were quite fluent in English in the Ugandan schools—never mind what they picked up while we were living in England! Now my son and daughter, who used to study and read at home, sit around watching TV! What can I do to convince the school that they need and deserve to be part of the gifted program?

If your school has a program for gifted kids but your child isn't qualified to take part, start by asking yourself: Does my district's definition of a gifted student include my child? If it doesn't, try to pinpoint precisely how the definition falls short.

If your child fits the definition but still doesn't qualify, ask yourself: Does my district's method for identifying gifted students discriminate against my child in some way? If it does, think carefully about where the school's methods fall short.

In the case where the school's definition and identification of giftedness exclude your child, you need to lobby on your child's behalf. Arrange a meeting with the gifted education coordinator or principal and the teacher. In your notebook, make a thorough list that shows the nature of your child's gifts and how he shows them at home: his style of learning, preferred intelligences, study and work habits, interests and passions. Also make notes about his cultural background and any other special learning needs you'll want to discuss. Bring your notebook and samples from your child's home portfolio to the meeting. Talk about your child's unique needs; ask the teacher what she's seen in the classroom that can support what you see at home.

Be prepared to compromise to some degree. For example, the curriculum coordinator or principal may be willing to ask the school board to change the definition of giftedness, but that could take several months. Ask if, in the meantime, your child can do some independent work, go to a different classroom for math, or get some mentored time in the science or writing lab or the art room. Willingness to take small steps may help you win the support of the gifted education coordinator or the teacher. Together, you can make additional progress a step at a time.

What If the Program Is Inadequate or Isn't Right for Your Child?

Unfortunately, many school gifted programs *are* inadequate. The challenge for you is to look at the situation as it currently exists, determine a strategy for raising the level of your child's education within the existing framework and, ideally, work with the school over time to improve what it has to offer gifted children.

A difficulty some parents face is that the program their school offers for high-ability students doesn't meet their child's needs. This is frequently the case for highly gifted and creatively gifted children. A highly gifted student (usually defined as a child who scores 150 or higher on an IQ test) may find a program unchallenging because his ability greatly exceeds that of his peers. An exceptionally creative child may be unhappy in a class with academically gifted kids who, as one child put it, "don't think in the same universe as me."

A child who turns in an entire script when a teacher asks the gifted class to come up with ideas for a play may need a more challenging program. One boy in an accelerated math program tried a completely new formula for getting at a mathematical law the group was learning. It worked. This boy was so creatively gifted that he couldn't tackle any assignment without putting his unique mark on it. He never felt satisfied until he'd discovered something new. Many teachers, even in gifted programs, find it difficult to respond perceptively to students like this.

Some programs don't provide focused, sufficiently enriched experiences for students with exceptional ability in specific subjects. A school may assume gifted kids are gifted in everything. However, if your child excels in math but works at grade level in reading and writing, she may struggle in a program that demands high performance in language and communication skills—as might a mathematically gifted child who has a learning impediment involving reading or speech. If this is the situation in your school, the focus of your advocacy needs to be to help the gifted education coordinator or teacher understand how the program is missing the mark for *your* child. One strategy can be to request that the classroom teacher create differentiated learning opportunities in the math curriculum.

Many schools provide no more for gifted kids than pull-out programs that meet for an hour once or twice a week.

> My son Gabriel got high scores on his achievement tests and his teacher recommended him for the gifted program. The program, which meets once a week, consists mainly of accelerated math, and Gabriel loves writing and art. He doesn't mind the program and he's doing okay, but it just isn't enough for him. Most days he's bored to death at school and comes home in a sulk. I don't want to seem ungrateful—at least he's getting something beyond the regular curriculum—but I'm worried about how this will affect his motivation in the long run.

Kids are gifted all the time—not just once or twice a week. If your school provides *some* services for gifted students, you may feel you have no right to ask for more. But you do. If the program or class doesn't work for your child, why should he (or you) just tolerate it? As a parent, it's your right and responsibility to speak up.

Teachers are trained professionals, but they don't *always* know what's best for your child. Regardless of your background or level of education, you are not necessarily less knowledgeable about gifted education than the teacher is. And you almost certainly know more about your child's particular gifts.

When the program isn't supporting your child, your first strategy should be to compare what you know about the program your child is in to what the district or state's policy calls for. If the state or district program goals exceed the services the school offers, make a note of what discrepancies you see. Schedule a conference with the teacher or other specialist who works with your child in the gifted program.

Come to school with as much information as possible about how the program falls short for your child. At your conference, start on a positive note. Thank the teacher for the program and mention something specific that your child likes about it. If the program isn't working in *any* way for your child, mention its benefits for other gifted kids. Then explain that while the program works well for some students, you believe your child needs something different. You can say, for example, "Our district's philosophy statement includes services for creatively gifted children, but the school's program seems to focus exclusively on academically gifted kids. Is there anything that can be done to encourage and challenge my child's creative abilities?"

Present evidence to support your words. Don't fall back on vague or faintly insulting generalizations like, "He never comes home excited about his gifted class," or "She's always frustrated because she wants to stay on a project much longer than the rest of the kids." Carefully avoid any statement that may sound like criticism of the teacher or the program. You want to create an alliance, not put the teacher on the defensive.

Bring projects from your home portfolio, school assignments, or anything else that shows your child's talents and learning styles. Say that you think your child is having trouble with the gifted program because of his individual needs and abilities. Ask for the teacher's suggestions and provide your own.

For example, suppose your child is unhappy about being pulled out of his regular classroom because he misses a lot and sometimes gets double homework. You might meet with the pull-out teacher and ask:

- Would it be possible for you to work with my child in his regular classroom at times?

- Would you consider helping his regular teacher compact the curriculum where that would be appropriate for my child? Could you help the teacher design independent projects and creative activities that will challenge my child without removing him from the classroom?

- Could you work with the classroom teacher to be sure my child isn't getting double homework or missing important or fun activities?

- Could you and my child's regular teacher see if the work my child does for you can replace certain classroom assignments?

What If There's No Gifted Program at All?

If your district doesn't officially recognize gifted students, talk to other parents, the principal, and the teacher to find out why. Be aware of the language you use. Some teachers expect parents who think their kids are gifted to be pushy and obnoxious. Until or unless you know how the teacher feels about educating gifted students, talk about your child in terms of her particular needs without mentioning the term "gifted." Suggest ways the school might provide for these needs. Show or describe examples of her work as evidence of what she can do.

Avoid generalizations that use the words *always* or *never*. ("She's always frustrated." "He's never excited about school.") Don't choose words that could reflect negatively on the teacher, such as *bored, repetitive,* or *uninteresting*. Rather than presenting your child as a brilliant student in a dull class, address the specific areas where your child's needs may differ from other children's. If you focus on what your child needs, rather than on ways the school or teacher is failing, you'll probably find much more openness to change. Look for common ground. This can be an especially good strategy if your district or school tends to regard gifted education as elitist.

My son Jake loves math. I showed his teacher a project he did in a summer math program for gifted students. I didn't say it was for gifted students, because there's a lot of resistance to gifted education in our school. Mrs. Jensen was surprised by the problems Jake had worked on. I said that I wasn't trying to push Jake, but that he often expressed a desire to learn and do more—and he felt he already knew most of what's in this year's textbook. Mrs. Jensen said she'd noticed that math came easily to Jake. She was willing to let him pretest out of each chapter as they worked through it in class. But she wasn't sure how to provide an alternative program for him. We talked further and decided to ask the curriculum coordinator for some ideas. This is just a start, but I feel confident that we're on the right track to help my son develop his talent. He's thrilled to know he can skip the stuff he knows and move on in a subject he loves.

Another strategy can be to investigate what's being done at school to help other groups of kids with special needs. Ask parents and teachers involved in those efforts for suggestions that might help in creating opportunities and programs for gifted children. A lack of services doesn't always mean the school has taken a hostile stance toward gifted education. It doesn't necessarily mean there's a lack of interest, either. Some schools are in isolated or remote areas, where it can be difficult to find staff or where there's no easy access to enrichment opportunities. Most schools can't provide gifted programming without state funding. Districts sometimes must compete with each other for state grants. But none of these reasons has to mean gifted kids can't get the challenge and stimulation they need. On investigation, you may discover an openness to your concerns for your child and a willingness to consider the problems faced by gifted students.

Sometimes a parent's interest can be the spark that ignites a school to look for creative ways to serve gifted children. A principal in Chicago whose two schools had no services for gifted kids responded enthusiastically when, on the suggestion of a parent, I invited his gifted students to participate in a summer program for talented urban and suburban children at The Center for Gifted. He visited the program and gladly helped arrange for kids from his schools to take part. In doing this, the principal gained some insight into ways of serving gifted kids. The biggest impact of the program was on the children themselves. The experience opened their eyes to many ways they can use and develop their exceptional talents and abilities.

If your school can't or won't provide appropriate services for its gifted and talented students, you may be able to create opportunities for your child in partnership with the classroom teacher. Knowing about instructional options such as curriculum compacting, independent study, and flexible grouping (described on pages 74–80) will help you talk knowledgeably with the teacher about realistic and affordable ways to challenge your child. Teachers vary in their familiarity with methods and materials suitable for gifted kids. If you share what you've learned in a respectful manner, many teachers will be interested and receptive. You might say:

- "My child loves your math class and wants to do more. Could she possibly do an extra project on number relationships? I know you have a lot of students to deal with, but I'd be happy to help. Maybe I could try to figure out a way to keep track of an independent project that won't involve much extra work for you."

- "My son Levi loves your English class, especially the reading response assignments where the kids analyze and write about literature. But he read and did a project on *Island of the Blue Dolphins* two years ago. My wife showed him a chapter from *Moby Dick*, and he and his friend Tyler were fascinated. I was wondering if he could work on a section of that book, or another book, instead. Would it be possible for Levi and Tyler to work together on a different reading and writing assignment for this unit?"

Offer the teacher whatever practical help you can. Often teachers are short-handed and overburdened and may welcome an offer of support. If your home library has pertinent books or articles, share them. Volunteer to do research and gather resources. Let the teacher know if you can serve as a classroom aide for high-ability kids or assist with a pull-out program. Help the school compile a list of other parents and community people willing to come in as volunteers and work with gifted children. Investigate places in the vicinity that would welcome small groups of gifted kids for hands-on experience in different pursuits. You might find interest at museums, arboretums, zoos or animal shelters, publishing houses, research labs, computer companies, theaters, or farms. Offer to do the phoning and paperwork necessary to set up these off-site experiences.

If you're concerned about your child's daily instruction and feel that teachers need training in differentiating curriculum, consider taking the lead in arranging a workshop for teachers in your school. Contact your state gifted association, state parent association, NAGC, or a nearby college or university to see who might be willing to conduct such a workshop for a reasonable fee.

Discuss these possibilities with your child's teacher, the gifted education coordinator, the principal, and anyone else you think may be interested. Sometimes getting one or two enthusiastic teachers excited enough to "talk up" an issue can be the catalyst that gets most of the school on board.

When you meet with the classroom teacher, ask how you can help provide more challenging work for your child. Explore different options. Ask about allowing your child to test out of material he's mastered. Talk about possibilities for independent projects, a mentorship, or a community enrichment program. If your child has exceptional talent in a particular area, such as writing or designing, show the teacher examples of his work and discuss ways he might continue to develop his ability.

Working with the School: Find Out More

Parent Education: Parents as Partners by Dorothy Knopper (Boulder, CO: Open Space Communications, 1997). This book presents an overview of parenting gifted children, as well as an understanding of giftedness and its unique characteristics. It provides support, understanding, and resources for parents as they facilitate the development of their children. It is also available in Spanish.

Take a Stand!

Take some time at this point to do a reality check about your child's situation and what the school has to offer.

- Think about what's working well for your gifted child in school and what isn't.

- Consider what and how much you think the school can reasonably be asked to do to improve your child's opportunities at school.

- Ask yourself what you can do before talking to anyone at school to prepare to advocate for your child.

Then schedule a meeting with your child's classroom teacher—or with the resource teacher, the middle-school advisory teacher, or a particular subject-area teacher. Plan to go to the meeting prepared to learn what you can and help the teacher learn more, too. Have in mind two or three specific ideas that might help improve what's happening for your child.

Before you go to this meeting, read the next chapter for strategies you can use to make your conference an effective one.

Chapter 8

Advocacy Is . . .
Getting Involved in Your Child's Education

I can't believe my dad. Without even telling me, he came to school and talked to my teacher—and the principal—about how bored I am in class because the work's so easy. Today Mr. Owens took me aside and gave me an extra math assignment. I was so embarrassed! The other kids were whispering, and I know they think I'm weird. I wish my dad hadn't complained. Mr. Owens doesn't like me anyway, because sometimes I do assignments my own way. I still get the right answer, but he thinks I should do the work the way he tells us to.

—Shane, grade 6

The first I heard that Shane's father was unhappy was when my principal called me in to say he'd been to see her. She told me I should meet with him and come to some sort of agreement about Shane. Why does she assume I'm not giving Shane what he needs just because his father (who's never been in my classroom) says so? If the father had questions about how Shane's doing in school, why didn't he come to me first? I like Shane—he's a bright kid. But he hardly ever follows directions, and he misbehaves a lot. Parents would find teachers a lot more receptive if they showed some appreciation of what we have to deal with. This year in my class I have four students with ADHD and six who barely know English. I work late every night planning lessons for thirty kids with different abilities and needs. Sometimes it seems that nothing I do is enough!

—Shane's teacher

Well, I've done it now—both my son and his teacher are mad at me. I was upset about Shane: his schoolwork doesn't challenge him, and he thinks Mr. Owens doesn't like him. So I talked with the principal. I told her how Shane finishes his homework in class while Mr. Owens presents material to the other kids that Shane already knows. I asked what the school's policy was on teaching gifted kids, but all she said was that she'd talk with Mr. Owens. Since I didn't get very far with the principal, I scheduled a conference with Mr. Owens myself. The meeting didn't go well. He got defensive right away because I'd complained (his word) to the principal. That wasn't what I meant to do—I just wanted some information. Then he said that even though Shane is bright, he's also disruptive and needs to learn how to follow directions before he gets any special privileges. I'm not asking for special privileges—just the education Shane needs. I left with nothing resolved, wondering where I'd gone wrong. Now Shane's getting extra homework that's just as boring as what he does in school, he's embarrassed about what the other kids think, and he's more convinced than ever that the teacher doesn't like him.

—Shane's father

Working with your gifted child's school can seem like a very tricky business. You're concerned, maybe even angry, but you don't want to alienate the very people you're hoping will help you. And the last person you want to upset is your child.

The experience of Shane, his father, and his teacher might have been more positive if Shane's dad had followed three basic steps for school advocacy:

1. **Talk first with your child.** To find out specifically what's happening for your child in school, the first step is to listen to your child and understand his feelings, fears, and frustrations. You need details as well as ideas from your child about what he thinks might help.

2. **At school, always begin by talking with the teacher.** Put yourself in the teacher's position. Wouldn't you prefer that a client or customer talk to you about a problem the two of you are having rather than go directly to your supervisor? Teachers feel the same way. No one appreciates being stepped over without even having a chance to talk about what's going on.

3. **Move "up the ladder" only after a good-faith effort with the teacher.** If it's clear that the teacher is unable or unwilling to help, then it's time to talk to someone higher in the school hierarchy.

TALK WITH YOUR CHILD

At every point in your advocacy, consult with and listen to your child. Be sure you're up to date on what's happening for her in the classroom—and what's not. If the opportunities your school offers don't seem to be right for her, talk with your child about precisely what doesn't work. Gifted kids can often describe their school experiences quite eloquently and in detail. Your child's perceptions and assessments of what's going on should be part of any discussion you have with school staff. You'll be in the best position to work for change when you know intimately what your child is experiencing and feeling.

I had made an appointment to meet with my daughter Surika's teacher. I told Surika that the teacher said on the phone she didn't feel Surika needed more or different work to do in class. Surika was indignant. She said, "But I already know all the stuff we're studying. School for me is just one long waiting room." One long waiting room—wow. That gave me the image I needed to focus my conversation with the teacher.

Your child needs to trust that you'll work in her best interests. To build that trust, help your child know that you want to understand and will think about her point of view.

Get the Specifics

Try to talk to your child about her day when she gets home from school. If that's not possible, plan another regular time to do this daily. Use this time to learn what the school day brought that was fun, disappointing, stimulating, or frustrating.

- With a younger child (kindergarten through second grade), one of the best ways to find out what's going on in the classroom is to look through her backpack with her. Kids love having something to show and explain. When you say to your child, "What's this all about?" or "Tell me about this," you'll often get more details.

- An older child might enjoy keeping an activity log. The log can be a good starting point for discussing what's happening in school. It can also give you a snapshot of the kind of work your child is being assigned and whether the teacher is adapting or varying classwork to fit your child's learning needs and abilities.

Read over the material, looking at the level of difficulty. How does an assignment compare with what you know your child can do? Do assignments call on her to do more than simple memorization? Does her work ask her to master a skill? Understand and apply a rule? Analyze a process? Create a new idea or an original way of doing something? Get your child's opinion about her textbooks and other written material. Which are fun to read? Which are too easy or repetitive? Which lead her to think more deeply about something? After talking with your child, make a few notes about what you've discussed so you'll have examples of what she's told you when you talk to the teacher.

Exploring the situation with your child will help you assess the seriousness of the problem. Even in the most ideal setting, there will be times when your child complains about a particular teacher, activity, or circumstance. Not every complaint requires a trip to the school or even a phone call. If you run to the school every time your child has a bad day, you risk gaining a reputation as a "hysterical" parent—something that will definitely work against your advocacy. So choose your campaigns wisely. Try first to resolve the problem by talking it over with your child and figuring out a plan together. If that doesn't seem to be working—if the situation is ongoing and seems to be making your child feel negative about school—you'll want to schedule a conference with the teacher.

Look at Behavior

Another way to gauge how school is going for your child is to consider behaviors, both those reported by the teacher and those you've noticed at home. A child may be struggling in school if she:

- resists going to school

- often has or complains of physical problems such as sleeplessness, stomach upsets, fatigue, or stress

- has trouble paying attention

- fools around in class or acts smart-alecky to the teacher

- doodles, daydreams, or mentally "checks out"

You can get lots of information by observing your child's behavior as she gets ready for school, after she comes home, while she's doing homework, and when you ask her about her day.

Tell Your Child What You Plan to Do

Gifted children want to be included in decisions involving their education and future. If, after you and your child have talked, you believe a conference with the teacher is called for, tell this to your child. If the idea of a conference worries her for any reason, see if there's a way to resolve her concerns. A child may struggle with feelings of being different, worry that the teacher will be mad, or just not want to "rock the boat" in school.

Consider Shane, whose father went to the principal and the teacher without consulting his son. Shane thinks his teacher doesn't like him. Shane's dad needs to find out why. He might broach the subject while he and Shane are doing something together, asking:

- Why do you think he doesn't like the way you do assignments? Did he say something? Does he ever tell you he likes your work?

- Why do you think Mr. Owens doesn't like you?

- Do you think he liked your work at the beginning of the year? What do you think happened to change his opinion?

Kids sometimes fear that the teacher will be mad at them if their parents speak out on their behalf. Some worry that their teacher's feelings will be hurt.

Hannah, my precocious second-grade daughter, was unhappy because her school work wasn't interesting for her. But she was dead set against my arranging a conference with her teacher. She told me, "Mom, I don't want Ms. Nguyen to think I don't like her. She has lots of problems with the kids in our room. They're always jumping up from their seats. She has to yell a lot, and sometimes she looks sad. If you tell her I said school is too easy, she might think she's a bad teacher and quit." Hearing this, I promised not to say Hannah was bored or didn't enjoy school. I told Hannah I'd start the conference by mentioning some of the things Hannah likes: book circles, the window garden, math games. "After that," I told her, "I'll talk with Ms. Nguyen about letting you do different activities when the class is studying things you already know." We talked together about what these activities might be. Hannah thought maybe she could read her own books, write stories, or do independent science projects.

I went to the conference with a far more compassionate attitude than I would have otherwise. Just as Hannah said, her teacher looked quite worn out and a little overwhelmed. It turns out she's a second-year teacher and has a number of challenging students to deal with. I began our conversation with what Hannah likes about school, just as Hannah and I had discussed. I could tell Ms. Nguyen was relieved I wasn't a bulldozer mom with a list of complaints. The meeting was productive and opened up a number of possibilities. She agreed to pretest Hannah to see which material she'd already mastered. She also suggested asking a fifth-grade teacher to mentor Hannah in science, her favorite subject.

By considering her daughter's concerns, Hannah's mother was able to reassure her *and* plan more knowledgeably and perceptively for the meeting with the teacher. Like this parent, when you ask your child how she'd like you to approach her teacher, you show her that you respect her feelings and insights. Let her know that you intend to proceed in a way that's comfortable for her. Keep in mind that an important long-term goal of your advocacy is to help your child take charge of her own individual school experience. Consulting with your child in this sensitive way is part of this process. By doing so, you allow her to participate in her own learning. You show her how to support her own talents in a productive, selective manner.

ARRANGE A CONFERENCE WITH THE TEACHER

The person most closely connected with a child's school experience is the classroom teacher. In your advocacy, this person is your first, and most likely your best, lifeline and potential ally. In some cases, you'll want to work instead, or additionally, with the gifted resource teacher or a teacher in a particular subject area.

Most parents attend conferences with teachers. They listen to the teacher's evaluation of their child's performance. They're shown classroom evidence of their child's work. They get a sense of what needs improvement. Advocacy conferences are a bit different. Usually an advocacy conference is:

- initiated by a parent

- used to present the parent's evidence of a gifted child's unique abilities and needs

- called out of concern that a child's school experience isn't meeting those needs, OR in a proactive effort to enlist the teacher's support and cooperation in providing an appropriate education for the child

When you call the teacher, ask to set up a meeting to discuss some aspects of your child's school experience that concern you. You might say: "I was wondering if I might come in and talk to you about my son's work in biology. He likes the class, but he's already learned quite a bit of the seventh-grade curriculum on his own. Could we get together and discuss some options so that he can focus on new material or explore what he knows in more depth?"

If, like Shane's father, you previously got off to a clumsy start, apologize to the teacher and let him know you'd like to make a fresh attempt. You might say: "I should have talked to you rather than the principal. I didn't think things through carefully enough, and I'm sorry. Could we give this another try?"

Strive to sound calm, even if you feel on edge. You don't want to put the teacher on the defensive or cause him to dread the meeting. When you're relaxed and cordial, the teacher is likely to approach the conference with an open attitude and be more inclined to give you the time and attention you need. Don't try to get into the specifics of why you want to meet. Do ask the teacher to schedule enough time—at least a half hour.

Before the Conference: Getting Ready

The more prepared you are for your conference, the more you'll accomplish. Using your notebook, clarify for yourself what your goals are and what you want to discuss. Think in terms of your overarching long-range goals for your child's education, and what steps could help attain them.

Don't be overly ambitious for your first conference. If you go into the meeting anticipating that it will result in a whole new educational program for your child, you'll probably be setting yourself up for disappointment. Change usually comes gradually, in a series of small steps. What you can realistically ask from a teacher depends on the situation or climate at school, including the teacher's attitude and responsibilities, the available resources, and the degree of support in the school for gifted kids and their teachers.

From your own research, you probably know a bit about the culture of the school—what's valued and encouraged. If your school has very few resources and little interest in gifted education, it doesn't make sense to ask a teacher to design an entire alternative program for your child. Even if a school's gifted program is broad and well supported, you'll still want to begin with smaller steps. This will help you forge a bond with the teacher that will allow you to work together step by step throughout the year to help your child get an appropriate, challenging education.

Set a specific goal for the meeting. Your goal for the meeting should involve some sort of action. Here are several examples of goals parents might set:

- The teacher will talk to the school psychologist about having my child tested individually.

- The teacher will assess my son's reading ability. If my child demonstrates advanced skills, the teacher will allow him to read more challenging books.

- The math curriculum will be compacted so my daughter can move at her own pace.

- The teacher will review the daily lesson plan to see where there's time for my child to do independent work.

- The teacher will arrange for my child to spend more time in the science lab developing new experiments.

- My child will be allowed to do more challenging projects in language arts.

- My child will have a chance to do more creative writing and journaling related to personal impressions, projects, and activities.

- My son will have opportunities to combine his talent for drawing with his work in math.

- My daughter will be asked to design and carry out an original project that supports her interest in anthropology, such as imagining and creating a new culture.

Plan what you'll say. It's valuable to think through what you'd like to say to the teacher and even rehearse a little, particularly if you feel nervous about going to school. Take time to write down questions you'll want to ask. Your questions will depend on the issue you're addressing. For example, if your child's work at home far surpasses the kinds of assignments she gets in class, you might ask:

- Is it possible for my daughter to work on a more complex geography project than the one the rest of the class is doing?

- Could my child design a Web page, since she's already mastered the computer skills the class is working on?

If your child isn't achieving what he could in school, you might ask:

- How do you help kids who aren't achieving at the level of their ability?

- My son does his best work when he does hands-on projects. Could he do something that enables him to apply what he knows such as an experiment, a composition, or a diagram?

Questions related to curriculum and teaching may include:

- How do you emphasize problem solving and other kinds of higher-level thinking in your curriculum?

- What opportunities do you provide for high-ability students to work together?

- How do you encourage students to work on problems and solutions in depth?

- Do you think my child would benefit from more independent projects?

- What do you do to help a child expand and extend her knowledge beyond what she knows already?

Gather examples from home. Search your child's home portfolio for examples of her work you can bring to the conference. You may be tempted to share much of what's in the portfolio, but choose just a few items that will give the teacher a clear idea of the type and range of her ability. You can supplement these samples with photographs or a list of additional projects, artwork, or writings.

At the Conference: Meeting with the Teacher

In many ways, the role of a parent advocating on behalf of a gifted child is much like that of a diplomat. Diplomats need to understand the perspectives of those they'll be negotiating with. They have to prepare strategies for speaking to the various parties involved, know what language might offend, what lines of argument might further their cause, and so forth. They also have to creatively and skillfully reach for common ground—those principles or interests that everyone can agree on. Over time, they must recognize differences and patiently seek ways to resolve them.

Approach your conference as a parent diplomat. Strive for a calm, reasonable manner. Greet the teacher with confidence and a friendly attitude. Let her know by your words and body language that you understand the many responsibilities she faces and that you respect her efforts to meet the needs of all her students. Let your manner show that you've come to exchange information and insights and to see what can be done to get your child the education she needs. If you feel anxious, take a deep breath and smile. Keep in mind that the teacher may be nervous, too—your affirming attitude can help defuse any tension either of you might be feeling.

Begin on a positive note. Tell the teacher what your child's told you about favorite activities—science discovery time, field trips, free choice in the library, new problems in math. Thank the teacher for her efforts. Try to be specific in your comments. It's always encouraging for a teacher (like anyone else) to know that her efforts are recognized and appreciated.

Get to the point. Next, explain clearly why you've come. Discuss your concerns using examples from what you know about your child. Show the teacher evidence of your child's talents and abilities: projects, artwork, writing, experiments, investigations, or anecdotes about her home activities. Explain what interests her and how she learns best, based on what you've observed at home.

Gradually introduce the subject of modifying the curriculum for your child. Start with the one issue that concerns you most. For example, if your child is bored and frustrated with spelling and grammar drills and wants to work on her own writing, focus your discussion on that. She might enjoy writing free verse, descriptive narratives, biographies, or essays on world conditions. You might ask about involving the curriculum coordinator or gifted resource teacher in designing alternative projects and setting achievement goals for your child. Many teachers are used to conferring with these specialists about educating their high-ability students.

Start building a partnership. Teachers often hear complaints, but rarely solutions. You're a supportive, informed parent who wants to cooperate with a teacher's efforts by sharing information about your child, identifying a problem your child is having, and suggesting specific, constructive ways to solve it. An effective way to present your ideas is through questions:

- My son loves languages and wants to start reading in Spanish. Are there simple books in Spanish in the media center? Could he pair up with a student who speaks Spanish?

- My daughter loves science but is finding that she already knows some of this year's curriculum. Could she test out of material or work ahead of the class? Could she do a more difficult version of some experiments? Could she design new experiments?

- My son loves art. Could he spend more time in the art room, as long as he keeps up with classwork? Could arrangements be made for him to receive advanced art instruction?

- My child is a history buff and she's very interested in women's history. Could she work on assignments in that area some of the time? Maybe you, she, and I could sit down together and talk about possibilities for independent projects.

Whenever you make a suggestion and get a positive response from your child's teacher, be quick to ask, "What can I do to help with this?" Strive to convey this attitude: "I understand that you've only known my child for a few months and that you deal with many children every day. Here are some things I know about her that might help you."

Listen carefully. Pay close attention to what the teacher says. Listen to the way she describes your child, and read between the lines. What's said and not said? What's communicated specifically and what's implied?

For example, suppose the teacher says, "Your daughter is a good student, but she needs to pay more attention to her work. Her handwriting is terrible, her desk is a mess, and her assignments look beaten up by the time they get to me." You might discern two messages from this: that the teacher recognizes your child's ability and that she values neatness. To respond, you want to let the teacher know you understand her concerns while at the same time focus on what you feel is important for your child. You might reply, "I know handwriting and neatness aren't her strong points. She seems to skip over the need for order because she gets so excited about the activity itself. I'd appreciate some ideas from you on how I can work with her in these areas without squelching her excitement for learning."

You are a vital link to your child's success in school. A wise teacher knows this and will listen to what you have to say. A wise parent will listen to the teacher's observations and recommendations. Even if you're feeling anxious to "prove your case," take care not to interrupt or monopolize the conversation. Try to avoid creating a barrier (even in your mind) between you and the teacher. The teacher sees your child in the context of a classroom of children and often from the vantage point of years of teaching experience. She has observations and suggestions that are good for you to hear. You and the teacher can work together most effectively when you can be mutual resources for one another.

Seek consensus. You want to leave the conference having reached some consensus with the teacher on how to improve things for your child. To accomplish this, you may need to make compromises. A compromise isn't a defeat: it's a step forward from where you started. For example, you may not manage to have your third-grade child moved to fourth grade, but you may be able to arrange for her to study certain subjects with fourth-grade students. You may not be able to get the school to relax its test score requirement for admission to the gifted program, but you may be able to arrange some educational alternatives for your child, such as extra time in the computer lab or the chance to team up with another gifted student on some projects.

Don't compromise on the essentials—only on options or details to put these essentials in place. If your daughter is creatively gifted, don't agree to just have her "put" in an accelerated science class—unless the class will allow her to experiment and be innovative. If your son is highly gifted but is still learning English, don't accept without question a requirement that he wait until he's more fluent before he's allowed to take part in advanced math. Ask that he be allowed to study math now with other gifted students. Agree to have him in ESL classes as needed, but don't put his gifts on hold until he's more proficient in English.

Get your questions answered. Be sure to clarify anything you're uncertain about. As necessary, repeat back what the teacher said to be sure you've understood. Do your best to avoid the problems that can arise from simple misunderstandings—such as assuming a suggestion is a promise or an agreement is a commitment to a plan of action. Before you leave:

- Go over what the two of you decided and what will happen next.

- Think about the goal you set for the meeting. Has it been met? If not, have you made progress toward reaching it?

Don't judge the success of this first conference *solely* on the results. If the teacher isn't particularly receptive to your suggestions but you manage to get a commitment to help, your meeting has been productive. If you and the teacher have reached an understanding despite some differences of opinion, the conference has moved you forward in your effort to get your child's educational needs met.

Under no circumstances should you feel pressured into accepting a plan you're unsure about. If you don't agree with the teacher's perceptions of your child or of what would best meet your child's needs, say you'd like to think over what was discussed and get back to her. Don't react negatively or impulsively. Give yourself the time and distance to consider what you've heard. During that time, you can think objectively about the teacher's point of view and consider other ways to approach issues that concern you. Then arrange to meet again.

Was the Conference Successful?

You'll know your meeting with the teacher was productive if:

• Your child was the main focus, not the opinions or agenda of you or the teacher.

• Both you and the teacher listened to each other and considered each other's point of view.

• You negotiated for solutions that will meet your child's needs without disregarding the teacher's responsibilities or your knowledge of your child.

• You came to an understanding even if you had different opinions.

• You both agreed to work on a solution that will help your child *and* to continue working together.

• You both made commitments and scheduled actions.

After the Conference: Follow Up and Support the Process

A conference is a beginning. Be prepared to initiate follow-up meetings, phone conversations, and other actions to keep the process going. Make yourself a copy of any learning contracts or written plans for your child's work as a reference. Do all you can to support the teacher by making sure your child sticks to her goals and does what she's agreed to do:

• If your child needs to arrange to test out of certain material before she can do independent work, be sure she does that.

• If your child has a learning contract with the teacher stipulating what she's to do and when, check in regularly with her to see how she's doing.

• If the teacher has agreed to give your child more advanced books to read, check this out with your child, see what books she's being given, and talk with her and the teacher about how things are going.

• If the teacher has committed to letting your child work with other gifted kids on a project, ask your child whether this has happened and keep checking in with her to hear how the project is going.

Even if your conference was very encouraging, teachers are busy and things don't always get done as quickly as you might wish. Talk with your child often about her school experiences. Look over assignments and homework. Without nagging or expressing impatience, call or write to the teacher if the changes you thought would happen soon haven't come about.

Schedule a second conference if you need to. If your first conference didn't produce any results, or if the teacher hasn't followed through or responded to your calls, arrange to meet with her again. Maybe at your first conference you caught the teacher on a particularly hard or stressful day. Maybe you said things you wish you'd phrased differently. Think over what happened and see where you might try a new approach. Give the teacher (and yourself) the benefit of the doubt. Give your child the benefit of your patience and your willingness to meet the teacher halfway.

When Andrew was in third grade, he didn't make the gifted program because his verbal scores were a little low. But he's amazingly gifted in science, so I scheduled a conference with his teacher to talk about giving him more challenging work in that subject. I came all organized with some of Andrew's projects from home and a little speech about how fascinated he is with our telescope and how he's always needed to find out how things work. Mr. Goffman just harrumphed and said, "Well, I can't do anything if he's not in the gifted program." I tried to get him to consider the possibility of allowing Andrew to do some independent work or finding a mentor for him. You'd think I was asking for the moon. By the end of the meeting I slunk out of there, discouraged and embarrassed.

It took me a while to recover from this experience. First I felt humiliated, then defensive, then angry, and finally indignant. When I asked Andrew how things were going in school, he said, "Mr. Goffman's a good teacher, Mom. He's nice to me, even if he doesn't want to give me more to do in science. It's okay this way." But I knew it wasn't okay, so I decided not to give up. Maybe Mr. Goffman had just had a bad day. I asked Andrew if he'd mind if I went to see his teacher one more time, and he agreed.

Before the second meeting, I told myself, "Loosen up, Mom! Stop feeling desperate. Your son's entire life isn't on the line here!" The first thing I said to Mr. Goffman when I sat down was, "It's me again, the pill who wants to know if her son can do some independent work in science. I'm sure you're thrilled to see me." There was a long pause. He didn't look at all friendly, and I began to sweat. But then he smiled and said, "Well, I *have* been watching Andrew a little more closely, and he does excel in science." I relaxed from that moment on. I think he was relieved to see that I was a parent who could laugh at herself. I also made it clear that I wasn't trying to be difficult. "I'm not here to make trouble," I told him. "It's just that Andrew *is* advanced in science, he loves it, and he'd like to do more. As his mom, I feel it's my responsibility to make sure he's getting stimulated and challenged."

After lots of discussion we worked it out. Mr. Goffman arranged for the middle-school science teacher to work with Andrew. This teacher has helped Andrew develop independent projects, and she's allowed him to join her sixth-grade class now and then. Andrew's done some exciting, tough work under her guidance, and he's glad I kept at it. Even better, this arrangement may be expanded. The science teacher has so enjoyed working with Andrew that she's offered to mentor a small group of younger gifted students every day. I'm really pleased about this. Andrew isn't the only one who needs this kind of activity.

This parent decided to give the teacher a second chance. She was open, considerate, and willing to laugh at herself and listen. She kept her goal—more difficult and engaging work in science for her son—firmly in mind. Most important, she was persistent. It's hard for a teacher *not* to listen in the face of this kind of friendly tenacity.

Be assertive. At the second conference, try to explain your concerns more clearly. Suggest realistic options that might help your child. Keep your goals in mind, and don't back down if the teacher seems disapproving or defensive. You can have a hopeful attitude without being a pushover. You're not an adversary, and neither is the teacher. If you do encounter a defensive or stubborn personality, step back and remind yourself, "I'm a reasonable parent with reasonable expectations. I'm asking the teacher to give my child a chance to learn." Clarify your purpose for the teacher: "My child has a right to an education that's appropriate for her learning needs. I'd be shirking my responsibility as a parent if I didn't step in when I see this isn't happening. I want to work *with* you, and I'm willing to help."

While it's best for all concerned when parents and teachers are allies, once in a while the effort to do this can get in the way of your advocacy.

During the last week of second grade I met with Mrs. Christiansen, the teacher my daughter Tara was to have for third grade. We had a pleasant conversation. I shared some of Tara's projects, and we discussed her interests and needs. I scheduled a conference for just before school started in the fall, and we had another friendly conversation. When I didn't see much happening as a result, I scheduled a second conference where Mrs. Christiansen told me about new training she'd had in differentiation that would allow her to improve Tara's learning opportunities in class. After several more weeks, though, I finally had to admit that my conversations with Tara's teacher hadn't produced any tangible results for my daughter. Tara was becoming more and more resistant about going to school in the mornings. One day she came home crying because Mrs. Christiansen had made her sit in the corner for talking when she was helping another child in the class. I realized that I had let the situation go on too long because I didn't want to sacrifice the friendly relationship I had with the teacher. I was mad at myself and angry with Mrs. Christiansen.

After I cooled off, I made an appointment to meet with her. The conference didn't go well—she seemed very surprised and got defensive. I then went to the principal. After several separate meetings with the principal, Mrs. Christiansen, the curriculum coordinator, and the school counselor, I was able to have Tara placed in the other third-grade classroom. That teacher is better equipped to serve the needs of gifted kids because she has several in her classroom.

During my meetings with Mrs. Christiansen and other staff members, I kept emphasizing the fact that I wasn't trying to create problems or seem ungrateful, but that the situation had become critical. My child was working on things she'd mastered a long time ago and, as a result, was beginning to dislike school. I didn't want her to develop a negative attitude or become a behavior problem because she wasn't getting what she needed.

What helped me the most during this process was learning to stay focused on my goal of helping my daughter—not letting my advocacy disintegrate into angry venting. Also, I realized that trying to keep the peace with a teacher isn't always the best way to help a child.

It's important to strike a balance between friendly, cordial relations with your child's teacher and your focus on improving your child's education. Neither should have to be sacrificed but, as this parent learned, if one has to go, don't let it be your advocacy.

Teaching Gifted Kids: Find Out More

If you'd like more detail about ways teachers can meet the needs of gifted children, check out these resources:

Helping Gifted Children Soar: A Practical Guide for Parents and Teachers by Carol A. Strip with Gretchen Hirsch (Scottsdale, AZ: Gifted Psychology Press, 2000). Share this book with a teacher who knows very little about gifted education. A version in Spanish is also available: *Ayudando A Niños Dotados A Volar.*

Keys to Parenting the Gifted Child by Sylvia Rimm (Hauppauge, NY: Barron's Educational Series, 1994). Discusses ways to work with schools and deal with problems as you advocate for your child.

Teaching Gifted Kids in the Regular Classroom, Revised, Expanded, Updated Edition by Susan Winebrenner (Minneapolis: Free Spirit Publishing, 2001). A comprehensive manual on proven techniques and strategies for teaching gifted students, this book is helpful for parents who want to understand how a teacher in a regular classroom can do more for their child.

Teaching Young Gifted Children in the Regular Classroom by Joan Franklin Smutny, Sally Yahnke Walker, and Elizabeth A. Meckstroth (Minneapolis: Free Spirit Publishing, 1997). In this creative resource on identifying and programming for young gifted children, the authors demonstrate how to tailor the learning environment to meet young children's special needs. Includes an extensive reference section.

Dealing with Difficult Issues

Some situations make it especially difficult to work with the teacher. It can be challenging to talk with a teacher about a gifted child who doesn't demonstrate high ability in class, whose behavior has become a problem, or who has learning differences that call for remediation.

Underachievement. Kids underachieve in school for various reasons—boredom, low self-esteem, a desire to fit in with others, learning differences, unusual or unrecognized talents, or stress. A parent whose child shows very little ability, interest, or effort in school may feel foolish coming in to discuss the needs of his gifted child.

I feel bad that Jason hates school and says he's so bored. But what can I do when he never exerts himself and all his grades are average? At the last conference his teacher told me he never pays attention and seems half asleep. I just don't think she'd appreciate me suggesting that it's her curriculum or teaching approach that's off.

In many cases, underachievement *is* related to the teacher's style and approach: the teacher insists the child work at the same level and pace as the rest of the class on content the child already knows and has mastered. Delicate as this situation is, a parent who sees evidence of gifts and talents at home even though his child turns in average or below-average work at school needs to bring this to the attention of the teacher.

If you face circumstances like this, it's especially important to gather all the evidence you can of your child's abilities as you've witnessed them at home and in other settings. Your portfolio of his projects and your notebook of observations will help you organize your thoughts and present your case to the teacher.

If you're uncertain about whether your underachieving child is gifted, pay special attention to discrepancies between his potential—as measured by standardized tests, behaviors you've observed, and projects he's done—and his performance in school. If there's any question of a learning disability, talk with the school counselor, psychologist, or special education director about having your child evaluated. Examine your child's behavior, too. Does your child make excuses about unfinished work and poor performance? Seem apathetic about school and yet love doing projects at home? Express giftedness in sophisticated speech, leadership skill, and creative work—but not at school?

Talk with your child about what, specifically, he dislikes or finds difficult about school. Think about his strengths and interests, comparing these with what he's given to do in school. Look over his assignments. What might challenge him more or stimulate him to greater achievement? Independent projects? More choice of topics? More hands-on activities? More computer time? More opportunities to be creative? If possible, formulate your ideas on paper and put them in a sequence you can present to the teacher.

At your conference, be positive. Don't say that your child doesn't pay attention or work hard because he's bored and unchallenged. Instead, explain straightforwardly what you've observed about his preferred learning style, his interests, and his talents. Ask for the teacher's suggestions about ways to accommodate your child's needs and encourage his achievements.

Talk with the teacher about how various subjects are taught. Does she teach exclusively from the textbook? If not, what other materials does she use? What kinds of activities are typical for her classroom? Does she have students work in small groups very often? Does she ever group high-ability kids together? What's her strategy for helping children who aren't working up to their potential?

Speak frankly and specifically about your child's unexceptional perform-ance: "I think Mason will do better on his writing assignments if he's allowed to choose his own topic occasionally." Teachers are often open to suggestions and willing to make adjustments for a child performing below his ability.

Behavior problems. Parents usually cringe when they hear that their child is misbehaving in class. With gifted children, behavior problems can com-plicate advocacy. Some teachers may feel they're rewarding unacceptable behavior if they arrange for special learning opportunities for a misbehaving child. They may say, "When he starts paying attention and stops fooling around with his friends, I'll think about alternative programming." Even teachers who are generally receptive to meeting the needs of gifted students may focus primarily on a child's misbehavior rather than on his assets.

If a teacher reports that your child is misbehaving, the first thing to do is talk to your child. Don't accuse him or get angry. Show him that you want to hear his perspective on what's happening and help him figure out a way to solve the problem. Together, try to come up with a plan. Talk with him in specific terms about what's bothering him at school. Is he happy with what he's learning and producing, or is the work repetitive and dull? Does he feel he fits in with the other kids? Does he like the teacher? Does he feel at home in his classroom—able to be himself? How much time does he get to work with kids of similar ability? Does he feel he can talk openly in class discus-sions? To help your child, you need to understand what he's reacting to when he misbehaves. You want to let him know that, while you insist on him taking responsibility for his actions, you also want to understand his feelings and will try to get him the educational experiences he needs.

One effective approach to improve a child's behavior in school is to develop a learning contract between the teacher and student. The contract should include a description of a project or activity the child will do, what the child is expected to accomplish, goals to meet along the way, a timeline, and rules of behavior. If a child breaks the rules or fails to fulfill the contract, he loses the opportunity to do independent work.

Erica, my fourth grader, has always had a mind of her own. I never worried about her at school, though, because she seemed happy and was doing well. When I got a note from her teacher telling me that she'd become disruptive in class and was involved in a number of pranks, I was surprised. This wasn't the child I knew.

I asked Erica what was going on, and she said she was tired of doing the same things over and over. I told her that I'd see what I could do to make school better for her—but first she'd have to apologize to the teacher and start improving her behavior. Erica did this, and I scheduled a conference with her teacher, Ms. Belzer.

Since Erica's behavior had improved, Ms. Belzer was willing to consider some alternative projects and assignments for her. I shared some of Erica's stories and her journal full of botanical drawings and detailed notes on plants. Ms. Belzer was impressed, but concerned about supervising Erica if she allowed her to do independent work. She told me she has thirty-two kids in her class—and I had the sense that she was feeling overwhelmed.

I asked Ms. Belzer if a teacher-student contract might work with Erica. She liked the idea. Together we went over what the contract should include. I convinced her to allow Erica some flexibility with the timeline, in case she discovered something she wanted to pursue in more depth. I also assured the teacher that I'd supervise Erica at home and do whatever I could to help her succeed.

At home, I talked with Erica about my meeting. She worried that the contract rules would make her feel like she was "in jail." "How can I do these different things if I'm worried about getting in trouble all the time?" I explained that if she showed Ms. Belzer she could act appropriately and focus on her work, she might get more independence. She'd have to prove herself and win her teacher's trust. Erica agreed to try to do this.

Then Erica, Ms. Belzer, and I met to discuss possible projects. Erica had an idea, and she was just brimming over with excitement. The second grade was doing its rainforest project. Erica wondered if she could help them design their mural. She wanted to sketch the trees and other plant life and share her research on rainforest habitat with the younger kids. This wasn't related to the fourth-grade curriculum, but Ms. Belzer was impressed by Erica's enthusiasm and promised to talk to the second grade teachers. When she did, she found they were thrilled to have an assistant who knew so much about the subject matter.

Erica and her teacher worked out a contract, which included a requirement that Erica produce something connected with the project—a short story, a report, or a set of proposals detailing what could be done to preserve rainforests. So far, things are going very well. When Erica finishes her work or shows she's mastered material the class is studying, she checks in with Ms. Belzer, reports on what she's done on her project so far, and then picks up where she left off.

Erica seems to like the structure, and she loves the freedom to pursue her special interest. I knew we'd had a breakthrough when she told me, "Sometimes school's almost as good as home." And Ms. Belzer seems like a new person when she talks to me about Erica.

If your child is underachieving because he's bored and unchallenged, you may hear, "Your child just isn't doing the work." Be calm and objective in responding to this—an emotional reaction often detracts and distracts from your purpose and puts you and the teacher on the wrong footing. Realize that teachers are obligated to see that every student masters certain skills and completes certain work. It can be difficult to see a child who's not finishing assignments as anything other than a problem. Try to see the situation from the teacher's perspective. You might say, "I know he should be doing his work, but I think he'd do his assignments more readily if he knew he could go on to more challenging material after he finished."

A learning disability. If you know your gifted child has a learning disability, your job as a parent is to shift your child's and the school's attention from a single-minded focus on her disability to the potential of her gifts. Encouraging your twice-exceptional child in areas where she excels is very important. This doesn't mean minimizing the learning problem's effects. It means bringing a sense of calm to your child: You assure her that you believe she can meet the challenges she faces and that you will help her. At the same time, you keep her focused on developing her abilities and strengths.

Many gifted children become successful students despite learning differences that affect their reading, writing, speaking, or listening. So much depends on how parents respond. If you feel your child's teachers or the school's learning specialist are overemphasizing a reading or speech impediment, you don't need to accept their recommendations unquestioningly.

Find out all you can about the disability and how it affects your child's capacity to think and learn. There are learning specialists who focus on the educational needs of twice-exceptional kids. You might want to ask the special education director or school psychologist to make a referral. Advocate for a solution that addresses your child's gifts as well as her disability. Support the school's efforts to strengthen her weak areas by asking how you and your child can work on them at home. At the same time, encourage your child to use her gifts and pursue ideas and projects that intrigue her.

Adopt a calm, unalarmed attitude about your child's learning difference so she knows:

- She'll be fully supported at home and in school in her efforts to strengthen her weaknesses and to develop her gifts.

- She can learn about her disability, understand the help she needs to address it, and work to overcome it or make adaptations as a way of reaching her potential.

Our third-grade boy, Tim, had a difficult time putting even simple sentences together on paper, so we had him evaluated by a psychologist. We discovered that he was highly gifted in abstract thinking, particularly in science and math, and that he excelled in logic and analysis, but he had trouble in spelling, grammar, and phonics. He could grasp concepts quickly, but had difficulty with sequential thinking. His work was often messy and his handwriting virtually illegible.

The school had no gifted program, and the teacher recommended that Tim be placed in a special education classroom. We knew he needed special help but wanted his considerable gifts encouraged and developed, too. We advocated for Tim to receive special help from the learning specialist while he remained in his regular classroom.

At home, we worked to provide our son with the enrichment and stimulation he craved. My husband is an electrician and he sometimes picked Tim up after school and took him to his work site. I tutored him in writing, using his interest in science as a starting point. At first, I had him write short sentences describing observations he'd made about his dad's work or about the turtles and fish in his aquarium. I helped him with grammar and spelling and had him rewrite sentences with too many errors. Gradually, Tim moved on to short paragraphs, then to longer ones where he could describe in more detail what he had observed.

Working with both of us and writing about science helped Tim begin to feel more confident about his language skills. He learned to like writing a lot more when he discovered that if he said a sentence aloud first, he could write it more easily. His work with the learning specialist encouraged him too, and school began to improve for him. During a conference, his teacher told us, "When Tim puts up his hand to talk, I know we're all going to learn something new and interesting." We're continuing to help Tim, but we're at a different place now and feel we are all working together.

Difficult Situations: Find Out More

Uniquely Gifted: Identifying and Meeting the Needs of the Twice Exceptional Student by Kiesa Kay (Gilsum, NH: Avocus Publishing, 2000). This book presents information and strategies for all types of situations where gifted kids have learning difficulties.

Why Bright Kids Get Poor Grades and What You Can Do About It by Sylvia Rimm (New York: Crown Publishing, 1996). Discusses both family- and school-based issues surrounding classroom underachievement.

Dealing with Negative Attitudes

It's difficult to stay calm, open-minded, flexible, and patient when you confront negative attitudes about gifted education. Even schools that go to the limit to help gifted kids may alienate various staff members in the process. Listen to one teacher's perspective:

> In my school, the administration gets a little too intensive about gifted kids. We have a child in our school who is highly gifted, really off the charts in certain areas of the curriculum. The parents, teachers, and gifted education coordinator—plus a specialist from a university—all got together to hammer out an individual education plan for him. The child is definitely improving (he used to be a behavior problem), but it bugs me that we're spending all this time and attention on one kid. Think of the time and resources—is it worth it? What about all the other kids?

If your school or your child's teacher seems to have a strong bias against gifted education and that negative attitude is impeding your child's progress, I recommend that you not get into a debate about it. As always, stay focused on your goal. Talk about what your child needs to thrive in school. Provide evidence of your child's strengths. Be specific about how your child's current program or placement isn't working and what you feel needs to be done to avoid the development of a more serious problem.

Call the teacher's attention to something outstanding your child did for her class. You might say, "He worked really hard on this and never lost his focus because he was thrilled to be learning something new. He likes this class a lot, but because he reads so fast and understands so quickly, he often reads ahead and stops paying attention. Is there a way you could give him more advanced reading or more challenging assignments?"

Respect the teacher as a professional. Understand the demands placed on teachers. But remember that you're not asking for the world, or for personal privileges. You're asking for some adjustments that will make it possible for your child to learn, as every child has the right to do.

Do what you can to help the teacher understand the probable causes of your child's problems and negotiate with her for an acceptable solution. Steer the conversation away from any differences of opinion you may have about gifted education. Focus on your child and his educational needs.

Don't be hard on yourself if you weren't able to reach an agreement with the teacher. Feel good that you conducted yourself diplomatically, gave the teacher plenty of opportunity to respond to your reasonable requests, and avoided personal antagonism or attack. Contacting another staff member is the next legitimate step in the advocacy process.

WORK UP THE LADDER OF THE SCHOOL

If you've gotten to know your school's staff, you'll know whom to speak to next: the gifted education coordinator, curriculum specialist, assistant principal, counselor, school psychologist, or director of special education. If not, you might ask the teacher who else you could talk to. Or, if you know that a particular staff member has worked with your child and is sympathetic to your cause, start with that person. Otherwise, talk with the administrator who has the most influence on decisions affecting your child's education.

When you meet with an administrator, explain your dilemma without criticizing the teacher or emphasizing your disagreements. As with other communications with the school, stay as objective as possible, explain the situation calmly, and listen carefully. Be strong and assertive about what you know is right for your child, but don't let frustration make you defensive or hostile. Hostility often puts an end to any chance of negotiating.

Use your notes. Let your notes focus and structure your meeting. Administrators will take you much more seriously if you can produce dates and details of what has transpired between you and the teacher or other school staff:

January 10–Met with Ms. Graham. She promised "more advanced" work for Melissa in math and language arts.

January 10-31–Talked with Melissa, checked her assignments. No change.

February 9–Met with Ms. Graham again. She denied having made any promises. Said Melissa's performance in language arts had been declining and so she couldn't participate in the gifted program. I asked her to review her records again and get back to me within the week.

February 24–Still haven't heard from Ms. Graham.

Provide all the evidence you can gather that relates to your child's abilities—including any high test scores, outstanding projects, and items from your home portfolio.

If I'd just gone to the principal and generally spouted off—even if I quoted things the teacher and I said—I don't think she would have been as receptive as she was. Parents are always complaining about this or that teacher. But I had taken notes and was able to supply the principal with dates and specific statements made by the teacher about my daughter, as well as a list of everything I did to try and help. She saw that the problems were real—in fact, her whole demeanor changed when she saw that I was serious, not just venting. I don't think I could have made the same impact had I not kept track of everything as it happened—in detail.

As with teacher conferences, it's always best to come with some ideas of your own. Tell the administrator what you believe your child needs in terms of content (such as more advanced and sophisticated material) and process (such as activities that draw on higher-level thinking skills, problem solving, independent research, analysis, and imagination). Ask what resources might be used to help your child. Could the psychologist assess your child's abilities and behavior and make a recommendation? Is there a paraprofessional or a teacher from a higher grade who would be willing to act as a mentor in subjects where your child excels? Could the curriculum coordinator provide some assistance in designing alternative projects or assignments that are more appropriate for your child's ability and level of knowledge? Principals can be especially helpful in this kind of discussion, because they know all the professionals in the school, including each staff member's particular strengths and expertise.

Be sure to leave the meeting with some kind of commitment—something more than "I'll think about it" or "I'll see what I can do." If the administrator needs to inquire into a situation or do some research, ask, "When will you have a definite answer?" Agree on a time when you'll talk again.

Don't give up! Don't resign yourself to a no-win situation. Despite difficult circumstances, keep pushing for your child's right to be educated appropriately. That's all you're asking. You are requesting that your child not be perpetually reviewing things he already knows, or repeating and practicing skills he's already mastered. You are asking the teacher to give your child a chance to learn. Taking this kind of stand is integral to your role as the parent of a gifted child. The growth of your son or daughter as a thinking person is at stake—and your advocacy is critical to making this happen.

Assertiveness: Find Out More

Here are two helpful books to get you started developing assertiveness skills:

Asserting Yourself: A Practical Guide for Positive Change by Sharon Anthony Bower and Gordon H. Bower (Reading, MA: Addison-Wesley Publishing, 1991). This book helps you develop important skills to improve your self-esteem, present your ideas, and cope with stress.

Your Perfect Right: A Guide to Assertive Living by Robert Alberti and Michael Emmons (Atascadero, CA: Impact Publishers, Inc., 1995). This manual has step-by-step procedures, detailed examples, and exercises to help increase your assertiveness. It's also available on audiocasette.

Help your son or daughter develop assertiveness with this book:

Stick Up for Yourself! Every Kid's Guide to Personal Power and Positive Self-Esteem by Gershen Kaufman, Lev Raphael, and Pamela Espeland (Free Spirit Publishing, 1999). Real-life examples help kids build self-esteem, assertiveness skills, responsibility, and healthy relationships. A *Teacher's Guide* is also available.

Many parents find it hard to be assertive. Make a commitment to work on your own assertiveness skills so you'll be more comfortable and effective negotiating with school personnel. Look for community classes or workshops to help you build these skills, or develop them on your own with the help of a book, your partner, or a friend.

Chapter 9

Advocacy Is . . . Searching Out Other Educational Options

Now that my son Alex is in third grade and eligible for the gifted program, he's in a pull-out group three times a week for 45 minutes. They do special projects, get extra computer or reading time, and work on more advanced assignments within the regular curriculum. The rest of the time at school, Alex is bored stiff. When I asked the gifted education coordinator for guidance on how I can negotiate for something more appropriate for him, she seemed to think I was pressuring him. The truth is, he's pressuring me! Lately Alex has been saying he wishes he could just get out of school altogether. What I'd never dare tell the coordinator is that he doesn't even like the pull-out program that much. At this point, I'm not sure whether the problem is Alex (he can be picky, and he has a low tolerance for anything repetitive) or the fact that the school isn't equipped to deal with him.

Some educators—and some parents—feel that any program for gifted students is better than no program at all. That may be true in some ways, but kids in inappropriate gifted programs can feel as unhappy and out of place as gifted children with no program or services. They may wonder what's wrong with them: Why aren't they content doing what everyone else is doing? They try, but their minds keep pulling them off into other directions and pursuits.

If this is the situation facing you and your child, there are other learning opportunities you can seek out. Doing this can take time, but it's essential that you continue pursuing an appropriate education for your child.

While exploring other options, don't put behavior concerns on hold. As you seek other avenues for educating your child, don't put off addressing low academic performance, behavior problems, or social and emotional concerns. Whether you're working with the school or seeking other educational options for your child, your efforts will take time and will probably be ongoing. Even if you know an anticipated new setting or more challenging program will help your child, don't let that stop you from working with the school and your child on underachievement or misbehavior (discussed in Chapter 8) or on issues related to your child's relationships with other kids and emotional well-being (Chapter 3).

Should You Be Worried About Your Child's Mental Health?

Being deeply unhappy at school can place any child at serious risk, including gifted children who can be extremely sensitive. Unhappiness that seems unable to be resolved can sometimes lead them to apathy, despair, depression, or even violence. Here are some warning signs to watch for:*

- noticeable behavior changes that aren't temporary

- intense mood swings

- a pattern of increasingly lower grades in school

- withdrawal into a fantasy world for a sustained amount of time

- long periods of sleep

- lack or loss of appetite that continues more than a week or two

- rigid, compulsive behavior

- excessive anxiety

- extreme perfectionism

- frequent feelings of powerlessness or an ongoing negative view of the future

- negative behavior toward animals or other people

- a morbid interest in violence or death

Don't worry silently about behaviors like these. Consult with a school psychologist, counselor, or medical professional right away. If you're not sure where to go for help, ask the school social worker or call a crisis hotline listed in the Yellow Pages.

Explore other learning avenues. If the school isn't able or willing to provide the stimulation and support your child needs, there are several actions you can take. What you choose to do will depend on how your child is doing in school, how she feels about what's happening, and how she seems to be responding. Some options you might consider include:

* Adapted from *The Survival Guide for Parents of Gifted Kids: How to Understand, Live with, and Stick Up for Your Gifted Child* by Sally Yahnke Walker, and *The Gifted Kids' Survival Guide: A Teen Handbook, Revised, Expanded, Updated Edition* by Judy Galbraith, M.A., and Jim Delisle, Ph.D. (Minneapolis; Free Spirit Publishing, 1991 and 1996). Used by permission.

- arranging for someone to mentor your child

- seeking help through a local community college, college, or university

- transferring your child to another school

- homeschooling your child full or part time

FIND A MENTOR FOR YOUR CHILD

Is your child passionately interested in a particular subject or occupation? If so, consider arranging a mentorship. Look for a person with special expertise in an area that interests your child. A mentor should also be sensitive to your child's abilities and learning style and enthusiastic about the subject your daughter or son will be exploring.

To find a mentor, talk to your own friends, other parents of gifted kids, teachers at local schools and universities, businesspeople, members of professional associations, and people in local arts groups. Where you look depends on the subject your child is interested in. It's not always easy to find a suitable mentor. You may have to be creative in your search.

I had asked around but was having no luck finding a mentor to work with my thirteen-year-old daughter Olivia. A friend suggested I post a notice at a nearby college, so I put up an index card on the bulletin board of the political science department that said I was looking for a mentor to work with my daughter in political science. I also asked the administrative assistant in the department to put my "advertisement" in the department's newsletter, which the assistant promised to do. I left other index cards in the college library, the student union, and a nearby coffee shop. I also continued talking to friends, associates, a college professor I knew, and some friends at church.

One day I got a call from a friend of a friend. This woman, whose name was Liz, said she'd heard I was looking for a mentor. Liz was a graduate student in political science. Ordinarily she tutored kids who were having trouble in school, but she told me she'd love to work with a young person who wanted to learn more about her favorite subject. I asked her for references, and called my friend as well as the other names Liz had given me. Everyone I called told me they thought Liz would be an excellent mentor for my daughter.

Olivia, Liz, and I met to get acquainted and discuss what Olivia wanted to learn. She said she'd gotten interested in politics by listening to discussions her dad and I had at the supper table. She was fascinated with how elections worked—especially campaigning, polling, and the role of the media—and hoped someday to be a political journalist. My daughter and Liz seemed to hit it off, and the mentorship was formed. Liz and Olivia both had a wonderful time going through each week's news stories and developing projects that helped Olivia get a deeper understanding of the politics behind various current events.

This example suggests three characteristics of a successful mentorship:

1. **Parent and child must both like and feel comfortable with the mentor.** If you have misgivings, trust them. If your child doesn't "take to" the mentor or if they don't seem to make a good match, don't try to force the relationship. Keep looking.

2. **The mentor must be willing to follow the child's interests and support her talents.** There is no set sequence or program of study. The point of a mentorship is to support what the child wants to learn and do.

3. **Child, mentor, and parent should discuss and agree on arrangements.** When you're considering this kind of one-on-one arrangement, you, your child, and potential mentor need to talk about how the two will work together. Be sure to involve your child both in the planning stages *and* after the mentorship gets going. It's important that your child feel free to say, "I don't want to go in this direction. I'm more interested in this."

Mentorships are more common for middle and high school students than for elementary-age kids. Younger gifted children tend to be interested in many things, less inclined to focus on one particular topic for an extended period of time. There are exceptions to this, however. I've known younger children with a deep interest in one or two subjects. A second grader in the summer program at National-Louis University had an extraordinary passion for mathematics. His parents had trouble finding enough resources to keep him going. Through the program, this boy formed a mentorship with our math teacher, who teaches gifted junior and senior high students at a university lab school. It was a perfect match for mentor and student, and the mentorship lasted for a year. The arrangement helped the parents understand better what sorts of math projects their son was ready for. The mentor also helped them see how important it was not to settle for the regular school curriculum, which wasn't giving this child the instruction he needed.

Once your daughter or son begins working with a mentor, be flexible about how long the arrangement may last. If your child gets little stimulation in school and comes alive when her mentor arrives, keep the arrangement going for as long as your child wants. Feel free to end it whenever your child loses interest or moves on to another passion. You might be able to find a mentor who can provide stimulating activities and projects in more than one subject.

Mentorships: Find Out More

Multicultural Mentoring of the Gifted and Talented by E. Paul Torrance, Kathy Goff, and Neil B. Satterfield (Waco, TX: Prufrock Press, 1997). This book will lead you through a step-by-step process of identifying possible mentors, developing relationships, putting ideas into practice, and ending the relationship. An informative book on the value of mentoring for gifted children from all cultural backgrounds.

National Mentoring Partnership (NMP)
1600 Duke Street, Suite 300
Alexandria, VA 22314
(703) 224-2200
www.mentoring.org
NMP works through state and community partnerships to make it easier for mentoring to occur and to help parents find mentors for kids. The Web site can point you to a wide variety of mentoring providers in your city, including faith-based organizations, schools, businesses, community organizations, and mentoring agencies. If you don't find your state through the links at NMP's site, go to an online search engine and type in your state name and the word *mentoring*.

Peer Resources—Mentoring
1052 Davie Street
Victoria, B.C. Canada V8S 4E3
(250) 595-3503
www.peer.ca/mentor.html
The Peer Resources Network (PRN) is a membership-based service provided by Peer Resources, a nonprofit, educational corporation specializing in the development of peer, coach, and mentor programs. Their Web site provides information (even to nonmembers) on mentorship experts, hundreds of mentor program descriptions, tips and ideas, and links to articles and research on mentoring.

Finding a mentor offers an invaluable way to keep your child's interests alive and to inspire her to pursue what she loves. When they work well, mentorships can be extraordinarily rewarding to a child. They're especially good at reinvigorating a bored or underachieving gifted child. They're also great fun.

In most cases, mentors are unpaid volunteers—they do this work because they care about their subject and the students they work with. One situation in which a mentor might want to be paid is if the person is a college student. In this case, the cost is usually for supplies or materials and typically is minimal.

LOOK TO COLLEGES AND UNIVERSITIES

Colleges and universities in your area can be useful sources of information and programs. Most have departments of education; many include faculty members with an interest in gifted education. In my role as director of The Center for Gifted, I've received many calls from parents requesting information on helping their gifted children. When I can, I visit schools to observe children at their parents' request, suggest contacts for further testing, and help families make some informed choices. I assist parents (with the school's approval), and I act as an outside consultant both to the parent and to the school. Outside consultants are in a unique position to help because they're seen as more objective than parents and can negotiate between the family and the school. You may be able to find a university person who can help you in this way.

Further, universities or colleges sometimes sponsor programs for gifted and talented children. Be sure to inquire, since schools don't always publicize information on such opportunities. Even if a university doesn't offer a program for gifted kids, you may be able to meet with an instructor who can offer guidance on finding resources for your child. Many university people get involved in the local schools—you might interest the person you talk with in doing research at your child's school or in undertaking a project to help gifted students. He or she might also agree to do a workshop at your child's school or to assist a group of parents in creating an enrichment program in the community. University teachers have resources and connections that can be valuable to you and to your child.

CHANGE SCHOOLS

Sometimes, even after you've worked with school staff to improve your child's education, you're forced to conclude that a school is never going to provide the kind of education your gifted son or daughter needs. At that point, you'll want to consider various options for changing schools:

- **Transfer to another school with a better program.** Many districts allow school choice, so families aren't restricted to the school their child is presently in. Since individual schools can vary greatly in how they approach gifted education, you may find that another school has a more appropriate program for your child. Research other schools—find possibilities through your state gifted association, your gifted education coordinator, or your parent group. Visit any that sound promising (with your child, if you can), and see whether a transfer is possible. Such a change may require your child to be bused or driven some distance each day, but you may decide the improvement is worth it.

- **Look into magnet schools.** Magnet schools place special emphasis on academic achievement or on a particular field such as science, technology, or the arts. These are public schools designed to attract students from all over a district. Magnet schools often have waiting lists; if you like a school but aren't sure it's the right fit for your child, it's still a good idea to get on the list.

- **Investigate charter schools.** Charter schools are state funded, but run by teachers and parents instead of school boards. While they must follow a number of state requirements, they aren't subject to school district regulations. Charter schools are more popular in some parts of the country than in others—see if your area has one. You may find the philosophy and teaching staff of a particular charter school to be very appealing.

- **Look at private schools.** Visit the private schools in your area to see how they educate their gifted students. The cost of enrolling a child in private school varies depending on the school and how it's funded, but the price tag can be high. Inquire about scholarships, and sliding tuition scales—some private schools have funds for deserving students. Don't assume that a private school will automatically offer your child more academically than a public school can. Private schools, even those with challenging curriculums, may have rigid programs and insufficient flexibility for meeting individual student needs. This varies from school to school. Early in your exploration of a private school, ask what the teachers do to offer differentiation or other curriculum adaptations for gifted students.

  Private schools that focus on gifted education can offer a great deal academically and artistically to gifted children and young people. I have worked with several in my area and find that gifted children respond with enthusiasm to the quality of academic and creative challenges afforded by a committed administration and faculty.

Whether you're looking at a different school in your district or a private school, carefully evaluate what the school has to offer. Talk to the school administrator, the curriculum director, and teachers who might work with your child. Visit classrooms, and ask to be put in touch with parents whose children attend the school.

CONSIDER HOMESCHOOLING

Homeschooling means educating your child at home or outside the conventional school environment. Increasing numbers of families are choosing this method, and a significant percentage of those families are homeschooling their gifted children. The notion of teaching your child at home may be overwhelming, especially if it's a new idea to you. You might wonder, "How can I teach my child when I don't have a background in education? Where would I find the time to homeschool? My eyes glaze over when I look at algebra problems—how could I possibly teach my child math?"

Actually, those who homeschool gifted kids represent quite a cross-section of the American population. They come from all walks of life. They homeschool in a variety of ways—some full time, others part time (weekends and maybe one weekday). Some families homeschool cooperatively, with parents of varying backgrounds and interests doing the teaching on a rotating schedule. Approaches vary with individual children and may change over time.

Parents of gifted children who choose homeschooling may never have taken education courses or completed college—though most have made it their business to learn all they can about gifted education. Their credentials include love of learning, imagination, vision, an appreciation and respect for the interests and passions of their children, and a determination to see their children's unique strengths used and developed.

Homeschooling is legal in all 50 states, Canada, and many other countries. The National Home Education Research Institute estimates that there are between 700,000 and 2 million young people in the United States who are schooled at home. Policies and procedures vary from state to state, and you can contact your local school board and ask for the homeschooling regulations for yours. You may have to send a letter of intent to your state department of education informing them of your plan to homeschool your child. Regulations about assessing your child's academic progress also vary by state. Some states require an evaluation at the end of the school year, either by having the child tested in the public school or by hiring a certified teacher to test him individually. Be sure you know what your legal obligations are before you begin homeschooling. Some states have fewer requirements.

Benefits of Homeschooling

Homeschooling has the potential to greatly benefit a gifted child. Depending on your own daughter or son's particular abilities and learning needs, you may see several advantages to this approach.

1. **With homeschooling, children can learn in more depth and breadth.** Homeschooling permits much more flexibility than your child would have within the standardized curriculum of school. A key frustration of many gifted kids is that they rarely get to delve into a subject in depth. Just when they get really interested, they have to stop and move to something else. At home, they can keep going.

2. **Homeschooling lets you teach according to your child's learning style and preferred intelligences.** For the gifted child who learns best through hands-on activities, who needs to talk out loud in order to work out his ideas, or who has any other unique approach to learning, the regular curriculum can be limiting and frustrating. Some gifted students do best when they're given a project and then are left to work on it in the way they choose and in the time they need. With homeschooling, parents can act as mentors, providing suggestions and giving feedback when needed.

3. **In a homeschool setting, you can tailor the curriculum specifically for your child.** When you teach your child at home, you can expand a curriculum to include your child's special interests, hone in more closely on particular topics, or diverge into new ones. As home educator and writer Deborah Haydock observes, "Gifted children often have powerful 'callings' which, I believe, should be honored, despite how unusual they may seem. Having choice and control in our lives is important for all of us, and it seems very important for gifted children to follow their deep passions and needs."*

4. **Homeschooling can accommodate a gifted child's intensity and unusual sensitivities.** Many gifted students have a hard time fitting into the structure and society of the regular classroom. One third grader put it this way: "Say the class is a metronome. Well, I'm a polyrhythm."

By the time he was halfway through first grade, my son Tomás was considered a "behavior problem." Testing indicated that he was of lower-than-average intelligence and the school and doctor had recommended medication to control his hyperactivity. I refused to

---

* "Homeschooling the Gifted—A Personal Introduction," by Deborah Haydock. In *Understanding Our Gifted* 9:2 (1997), page 17.

accept this. At home, Tomás was lively but never out of control, and he loved learning about every vehicle that moves, from soapbox cars to rocket ships. I decided to homeschool Tomás. Today, at eleven, he's an excellent student and tests in the top percentile in his annual state tests. He doesn't miss his old school at all, and he now has a chance to try out many new ideas.

5. A homeschooled gifted child needn't feel isolated and out of sync with other students. Ironically, one of the main reasons some people oppose homeschooling is the supposed lack of socialization. Yet parents of gifted kids who are homeschooled report that their kids do fine socially, and I've seen this to be true in most cases. In some ways gifted kids may do *better* socially when they're homeschooled than when they're in a regular classroom. Homeschooled children often learn in multi-age groups, with siblings or with other students, particularly if several families homeschool together. These kids also form friendships in their neighborhood, at community events and activities, and in settings such as 4H, scouts, youth groups, athletic teams, and clubs.

Drawbacks of Homeschooling
There can be a downside to homeschooling, dependent again on the child, the situation in the regular classroom and school, and the way families go about educating their child at home.

1. Homeschooling is a big commitment. Perhaps the most obvious drawback to full-time homeschooling is the time and commitment it requires. While you're gathering information, think about your family. If your spouse or partner isn't happy with the plan, or if the needs of other children or other family members demand too much time and energy, you may conclude that homeschooling isn't the right choice. Remember that you'll have to work out a teaching schedule that suits your job and other responsibilities.

2. Some homeschooled kids miss the camaraderie of the classroom. Another potential drawback is that homeschooled children may feel "out of it" because they don't go to regular school like other kids do. Successful homeschooling depends a great deal on your child's needs and personality. While some gifted kids have problems socializing with their peers in school, others do not. Your child may make friends easily and enjoy being in school, even though he's bored and frustrated with the curriculum. He may be independent and like being away from home each day, with things to tell you that you don't already know.

Even though I think homeschooling would benefit my daughter in some ways, she just loves going to school with her friends. When she comes home, there are always other kids with her, and they sit around the kitchen table talking excitedly about what's going on in school. She likes working on projects in small groups with other kids, and she seems to thrive on the social aspect of school. I just can't take that away from her.

3. Schools are often better equipped to help young people who have LD or are learning English. Homeschooling isn't always the right option for a twice-exceptional gifted child. If your child has a learning disability or if he's not yet fluent in English, he may need the support of professionals at school.

Part-Time Homeschooling

If you'd like to teach your child at home but can't commit to doing so full time, think about part-time homeschooling. You might, for example, be able to work out an arrangement for teaching your child one afternoon or one day a week. Particularly if your school offers little for gifted children, part-time homeschooling could make a real difference in your child's educational life.

I had given up on ever getting the school to agree on a more individualized program for my lively fourth grader, Michelle. They'd accelerated her in a couple of subjects, and that was as far as they were willing to go. Michelle wasn't unhappy, but it bothered me that she'd lost that spark she used to have. School was just "okay."

I heard about homeschooling from a friend. It sounded interesting, so I sent away for information, read some books, and subscribed to a magazine on the subject. The more I found out, the more inspired I felt, but I knew I couldn't teach Michelle at home full time. I finally decided to try something out on a smaller scale. I used Michelle's schoolwork as a starting point. When we started this experiment, her class was studying the Civil War, so Michelle and I both read biographies of people from the period. We looked at Matthew Brady's photographs and read *Uncle Tom's Cabin*. Michelle got interested in Jefferson Davis, so she did research on his life. She loved this, and I began to see the old spark.

We kept doing this extra work at night and on weekends. Sometimes Michelle would share her home projects with her class. I showed some of her work to the teacher, who was quite impressed and began to think again about Michelle's special needs. With the teacher's support, the school agreed to allow Michelle to stay home with me one morning a week—I worked things out at work so I could do this. Michelle is also allowed to leave school early for special home projects. She knows she has to keep up with her regular schoolwork, but she's more than willing to do this.

If part-time homeschooling interests you, look first at your child's areas of greatest need. If your son or daughter is unusually imaginative, consider taking topics from the school curriculum and using them as catalysts for projects, as Michelle's parent did. You might also use the time to combine one of your child's special interests with a subject that's being covered in school. If your child is fascinated by space exploration, you could create projects that connect to science, art, or social studies.

You'll need to negotiate with your child's teacher, the principal, and perhaps the superintendent to arrange part-time homeschooling. A great deal depends on your relationship with the teacher and school administration. Your success in making this arrangement also depends on school policies. But part-time homeschooling might be a workable, enjoyable option for you and your child.

Try Homeschooling During the Summer

Consider trying your hand at homeschooling during the summer. With your child, decide on a theme or topic to work on. Go to the library, visit exhibits, nature centers, and parks. Check out Web sites that can stimulate ideas for research and activities. Offer plenty of opportunities for your child to *produce* something, such as an experiment, a piece of writing, a model, a painting, or a skit.

Like any educational option, homeschooling works better for some kids and parents than for others. Take your time as you consider the idea of homeschooling, researching it thoroughly and weighing all factors, pro and con. As you do, keep in mind that homeschooling needn't be an all-or-nothing proposition. Consider the unique needs of your child—social, emotional, and educational—and let these guide you.

Homeschooling: Find Out More

Homeschooling is an increasingly popular option for families, and you'll find many books, magazine articles, and Web sites devoted to it. Consult your library, board of education, state parent association, and the Internet. Every state and most Canadian provinces have homeschooling associations as well as support groups, annual conventions, and Web sites. Talk to homeschooling parents—they can answer your questions and give you a realistic picture of what's involved. You may find a local homeschooling parent group, too. Here are a few resources to get you started:

"Best of Both Worlds: Part-Time Public School and Part-Time Homeschooling for Elementary Gifted Children" by Carol Danz, in *Communicator,* Summer 1999. See page 175 for information on obtaining issues of this magazine published by the California Association for the Gifted (CAG).

The Complete Guide to Home Schooling by John and Kathy Perry (Los Angeles: Lowell House, 2000). This book can help you explore whether to homeschool, how to develop confidence and keep life in balance as a homeschooling parent, what curricula to teach, and how to approach homeschooling with elementary, middle school, and high school students. The authors also provide a comprehensive list of phone numbers and electronic addresses for departments of education and home educator organizations in all fifty states.

"Is Homeschooling Right for Your Child?" by Vicki Carvana, in *Parenting for High Potential* (September 1997), pages 12–14. Check at the library or on the Internet for this article, or contact NAGC (see page 62 for more information).

National Center for Home Education
P.O. Box 3000
Purcellville, VA 20134
nche.hslda.org
Founded in 1990 by the Home School Legal Defense Association, this organization provides resources to homeschool support groups and organizations. It serves as an information clearinghouse and monitors legislation that affects homeschoolers.

Association of Canadian Home-Based Education (ACHBE)
P.O. Box 34148, RPO Fort Richmond
Winnipeg, Manitoba R3T 5T5
www.flora.org/homeschool-ca/achbe/index.html
ACHBE provides support, advice, and information on homeschooling to individuals and organizations, including legal support. The Web site lists contacts by province.

Take a Stand!

Think carefully about what's going on for your child in school. Are her learning needs well met? Are you satisfied with how the teacher and school work with you to provide appropriately challenging experiences for your child? Could your child benefit from a mentor? An out-of-school program? Would it be worthwhile to explore the possibility of changing schools, or of homeschooling full or part time? Talk with your child about opportunities beyond the school and classroom she's presently in. Then take the initiative to seriously begin exploring an option that could offer your child more or better learning opportunities.

Part 3

Moving Into the Community and Beyond

As concerned as you are about your gifted child's education, the issue often goes beyond the experience of your individual son or daughter. In many schools and districts, gifted students are simply not receiving the services they need. When you act on behalf of your child, you can open the doors for other gifted kids as well.

The most effective parent advocates are those who have a clear commitment to gifted education, a goal that's larger than "fixing the situation for my child." This attitude can help lessen charges of elitism and self-interest that parent advocates sometimes run into. You needn't become the guardian angel of all gifted students, but it's important to balance your specific goals for your child with the overall issue of the right of *all* gifted children to an appropriate education.

To accomplish change for gifted kids, it's often necessary to take your advocacy beyond the doors of the school. There are many avenues to follow: You might get to know another parent of a gifted child so you can share ideas and strategies. You might join, or even start, a parent group so that you can work collectively to influence your school's or district's policies. You might even decide to lobby your legislator—or your state's legislative body—to change the laws that direct gifted programming and to increase funding for schools.

In Part 3, you will explore these and other ways to take your advocacy into the greater world and make a difference for all gifted children and young people. You'll also consider things you can do to make sure your advocate's role doesn't overwhelm you or keep you from making time to pursue your own interests and renew your spirit.

Chapter 10
Advocacy Is . . .
Connecting with Other Parents

My seventh-grade son Tyler has always been a good student, but *not* because of anything the school does. Our city's district is large, and so many kids need help with basic skills that the needs of gifted kids aren't seen as any kind of priority. Tyler's teachers don't seem to expect anything exceptional from him, and now, in his second year of middle school, he's losing his motivation and his grades have begun to slip. I've tried to work with some of his teachers, and I've talked to the principal, but they've basically told me I should just be glad that most things "come easy" to Tyler.

A few weeks ago, three other parents and I asked for a meeting with a group of teachers and the principal. As we listened to the teachers explain all they have to deal with in the classroom, we could see they were overloaded and overwhelmed. At the end of the meeting, we asked if any teacher wanted to work with us to figure out *some* kind of arrangement for grouping the gifted kids together for advanced-level work. No one responded, but two days later one of the teachers called me and said one of the high-school science teachers was interested in working with a group of gifted kids. She said she'd talked to the curriculum coordinator about hiring a part-time paraprofessional to work with this teacher. We are pleased that a couple of people at school finally seem to have heard us and that they're willing to work something out. We don't want to stop here, though—we know our kids need more stimulating opportunities in their regular classrooms, too.

Our school has no special programming for gifted kids. I've talked with teachers, the curriculum director, and the principal—we just don't agree about what my daughter Chantel needs to develop her abilities. Right now, I can't move her to a different school, and homeschooling isn't an option for me. A friend in a nearby town, whose son is gifted, told me she and her husband meet regularly with a small group of other parents. They share ideas and information, and they've also presented recommendations to their school board.

I decided to reach out to other parents, too. I posted signs about a meeting for parents of gifted kids. Only two people showed up; even so, we had a lively discussion about what our kids need and how we might work with the school or the district to improve gifted services. We attended several school board meetings and felt that one or two members might be receptive to our cause. One proved particularly sympathetic and advised us on how to present our concerns to the board. This person became an advocate for gifted and talented children and is pushing for some changes in the district's attitude toward gifted education. We've continued to talk with her, and we're confident that if we all keep working at it, opportunities will soon open up for our kids. We've also attracted more parents—now nine of us are working together.

It's worth repeating: Without the advocacy of parents, gifted education would not be where it is today. Many of the programs available to gifted young people exist largely because of the persistence of parents determined to see their children educated appropriately.

One of the most common problems faced by parents of gifted kids is isolation. It's easy to get discouraged when you feel you have no support, no one besides your spouse or partner, if you have one, to talk with about the challenges you're facing, and no way of gaining fresh perspective on your child's situation. In my seminars for parents, I'm always touched by the hunger that fathers and mothers have for information and encouragement. Some want to take action but don't know where to turn or how to begin on their own. Some fear they're not doing the right things or not approaching their problems in the most constructive way. Others have grown discouraged because their efforts to work with the school seem ineffective.

Whatever you do, don't struggle alone. Some of the most supportive people you will find are parents of other gifted students. People who understand the difficulties you face can offer practical advice and reassurance when you most need it; they can also add their voices to yours as advocates for change. And it's a fact of life that schools, school boards, and districts tend to listen more closely to groups than to individuals.

REACH OUT TO OTHER PARENTS

There are different ways of connecting and working with like-minded parents.

My daughter and I moved to a new district in September. Tia's been unhappy—angry about moving away from her friends and bored in school. She was in a gifted program in her old school, but this new school has nothing to encourage her interest in math and writing. Tia also feels out of place because there are fewer Mexican-American children at this school. She says the other girls don't like her. I talked with the teacher and principal. They both said the school had trained the teachers to adjust their curriculum for students above or below the grade level, but I don't see much evidence of this. Tia was just shy, they said. She'd adjust after a while.

I didn't see much hope for change until I went to a PTA meeting and struck up a conversation with another parent. It turned out that our two girls are in the same class. I told this mom about Tia's problems. She said her daughter Kirsten is also bright, but that she'd never pushed for changes at school because the school told her the same thing they'd told me—that they were providing for gifted kids in the regular classroom. She and I began working together. We made a list of what we thought would help our kids and went together to discuss it with the principal. He seemed more receptive than he'd been to either of us individually. If nothing changes, though, we plan to explain our situation to the school board.

It's great to have someone to talk to and work with! The other good thing that's come of this is that our daughters have become friends.

These parents met by chance and began an informal collaboration. PTA or PTO meetings and other school functions are great places to meet potential allies and friends. If you're feeling stonewalled working alone, you may be able to connect with another parent in the same manner. Another benefit of doing this, as Elena's mother found, is that when you begin forming networks with other parents, you may also find new friends for your child. Even if kids attend different schools, the families can arrange to meet—at a playground, a restaurant, a sports activity, or the library, for example. Your child may be thrilled to meet other kids with similar interests, energy, intellect, and imagination.

Not all campaigns for change succeed, but you may be surprised by the power you have as a group of concerned parents. Often, when parents have one particular issue they feel strongly about, they can accomplish a good deal by joining forces.

My wife and I joined together with other parents of third-grade gifted children to protest our school's identification procedures. Most of us immigrated to the community from the Philippines. Our children know some English, but not as much as their American-born classmates. We felt the tests used to select students for the gifted program, all of which required strong English skills, excluded our children unfairly. We knew our children had enough English to do advanced work in a number of subjects. All we wanted was broader selection—such as tests that more fairly measure talent in kids who are still learning English. When the teachers didn't respond to our concerns, we went to the principal, who was sympathetic but said the gifted program required a thorough understanding of English. He recommended that we present our case to the superintendent.

Fortunately, the superintendent realized that this issue had to be addressed—the district was enrolling more and more ESL students. He met with us along with the school psychologist and a consultant from a local university to discuss other tests for English-language learners. Eventually, the district added two additional tests for identification, both of which depended less on English-language skills. The district also decided to use portfolios of student work to measure ability. The results of this affected not only our children, but a number of other kids who hadn't scored high enough on the old tests. These kids as well as ours now qualified for gifted programming.

JOIN AN EXISTING PARENT GROUP

Many parents find the support and motivation that comes from working with an ongoing group to be extremely helpful for their advocacy. Groups for parents of gifted kids come in all sizes and can provide a variety of benefits including resources for information and networking, support for families, advocacy for policy-level changes, bridges between schools and families, and opportunities for parents and kids to meet others with similar interests and concerns.

Ask the gifted education coordinator or the principal if your school or district has a group for parents of gifted kids. If not, there may be a group that includes parents from various districts. Your state's gifted association may also be able to direct you to parent groups and activities going on in your area. (In some cases, the state association *is* the parent association, as in Illinois.) You might also contact a university education department that offers courses in gifted education and see if they have any information on parent groups.

If you find a group in your area, arrange to attend a meeting. Try to get a sense of the members' goals and see what kinds of activities the group is involved in.

What Makes an Effective Parent Group?

In seeking out a group for parents of gifted children, look for one that:

- Has a goal, purpose or mission statement, and bylaws that all members agree to.

- Is a democratic organization in which all members have a voice.

- Elects officers whose roles and responsibilities are clearly defined.

- Charges dues that are reasonable and that don't exclude any parent from membership because of financial hardship.

- Seeks out and welcomes new members.

- Meets regularly and follows an agenda.

- Shares information, resources, and ideas.

- Sponsors speakers, workshops, and programs on topics of interest to the members.

- Arranges activities that involve whole families.

- Regularly communicates with members through mailings, with a newsletter, or by phone or email.

Avoid parent groups that spend too much time complaining about a school's modest or nonexistent efforts to support gifted kids. Airing frustrations is a normal part of most parent meetings and has its place, but only in small measure. While you may feel relieved to meet people who understand and appreciate your struggle, continual gripe sessions where people do little more than reiterate negative experiences is counterproductive and can lead to working in a void. You'll want a group that has both a commitment to and an expectation of progress—a setting where you can share ideas and collaborate on efforts to change things for the better.

Join a Parent Group Online: Find Out **More**

The Internet is an excellent option if you want to connect with parents from different parts of the world or are seeking quick feedback on a particular issue. NAGC has links to parents groups, as may your state or provincial gifted association's Web site. Here are some other sites to visit:

Gifted Children Monthly
www.gifted-children.com
This online networking and information site is an offshoot of *Gifted Children Monthly*, an award-winning newsletter for parents of gifted children. Membership in the online organization is $10 per year. The site has a broad range of services including a newsboard, access to advisory boards and other experts, chat forums, and school briefs.

GT World
www.gtworld.org
GT World is an online support community for parents of gifted and talented children, providing an arena for discussing and researching advocacy issues. You can post questions or statements on one of its mailing lists and request responses from other parents. The site also has a chatroom, GTworldMOO, where you can talk in real time with other members.

Hoagies' Gifted Education Page
www.hoagiesgifted.org
This excellent resource offers online and print resources on various aspects of giftedness. It provides a comprehensive section on identification and enables parents to exchange information, talk to teachers, find out about homeschooling, and research schools across the country. Also check out Hoagie's site for gifted children and teens (*www.hoagieskis.org*).

TAG Family Network
www.teleport.com/~rkaltwas/tag
The TAG Family Network is an organization run by and for parents. The group disseminates information, supports parents, and monitors and influences legal issues. Membership is free. The Network's home page provides extensive links to online gifted resources, as well as information on enrichment programs, talent searches, and mailing lists. It's a helpful starting point for parents seeking information on a range of advocacy issues.

START A NEW PARENT GROUP

If there are no groups nearby, consider starting one. If you know other parents of gifted kids, call them and see if they'd like to join you in forming a group. Ask school staff members to help you pass the word to other parents. Solicit help from the PTA. Put up notices in the school library, in the children's and young adult's sections of the public library, and at your local community center. Place an announcement in the local paper. Get advice by connecting with parent groups in other areas, or call your state's parent association for guidance.

If your district has a gifted education coordinator, ask this person to help spread the word about your group and possibly to assist in getting the group organized. To ensure that it functions well, the group's goals should be well defined and its meetings carefully planned based on members' concerns and interests. By formalizing your group's organization and meeting structure and by addressing the specific advocacy concerns of its members, the parent group will more readily stay focused on its most important goal: to improve the education of gifted children.

Topics for Your Meetings

For your first meeting, you might have the gifted education coordinator talk about the district's program—the underlying philosophy and educational objectives, how it is structured and staffed, and how the funding works. For future meetings, members can suggest topics that concern or interest them. Such topics might include:

- characteristics of gifted children

- identifying and supporting specific target populations, such as young gifted children

- communicating effectively with the school

- social and emotional needs of gifted children

- parents as school volunteers

- projects and activities to do at home

- homeschooling

- parenting gifted children with particular needs (such as gifted girls, middle schoolers, learners who are twice exceptional, highly gifted young people, or English-language learners)

- helpful Web sites for gifted students and their parents

- school and district policy issues

- state legislative issues

Depending on the group members and the challenges you face in your district, other issues may emerge, such as how to improve identification procedures or what to do about funding cuts in the district. See whether your group might attend a workshop at a nearby university or hold its own workshop. Some schools and university-based gifted programs offer parent seminars that run concurrently with programs for children. Parents often use this opportunity to network and share ideas on advocacy.

Organizing Parent Groups: Find Out More

For information on organizing and participating in parent groups, see the following resources:

Gifted Parent Groups: The SENG Model, by James T. Webb and Arlene R. DeVries (Scottsdale, AZ: Gifted Psychology Press, 1998). This manual assists parents and others who want to form parent discussion groups. SENG (Supporting the Emotional Needs of the Gifted) groups help parents with the special challenges of raising gifted kids—emotional, social, and educational.

"Guiding the Parents of Gifted Children," by Elizabeth A. Meckstroth, in *Counseling Gifted and Talented Children: A Guide for Teachers, Counselors, and Parents,* edited by Roberta M. Milgram (Stamford, CT: Ablex Publishing, 1991), pages 95–120. Meckstroth's chapter offers practical information for parents on how to set up and facilitate discussion groups.

The Parent's Handbook: Systematic Training for Effective Parenting (STEP) by Don Dinkmeyer Sr., Gary D. McKay, and Don Dinkmeyer Jr. (Circle Pines, MN: American Guidance Service, 1997), pages 16–26. This guide, which supports the STEP parenting program, describes how to facilitate parent groups and discusses group dynamics including leadership skills, information about confidentiality, and practical suggestions for dealing with problems such as members who monopolize discussion. Before going to the expense of ordering the guide, see if your school, community education program, library, or place of worship has one that you can check out.

Parents Can Effect Real Change

Working with like-minded parents can help you feel less alone and better informed. You'll see clearly that you can make a real difference in your child's life. No longer are you an isolated individual struggling to improve things for your own child. Now, when you present your case to the board of education or talk with an administrator, you are representing all the gifted students in the district and their families.

As an example of how parents can join forces to improve the education of gifted kids, consider the experience of this group of parents in Illinois:

Four parents met in the school library to discuss the gifted program. Because the program was underfunded, the gifted education coordinator (who was also the teacher) had to travel among three elementary schools in the district. The pull-out program she provided wasn't particularly challenging, and students complained about missing work in their regular classroom.

The parents drew up a plan: They would meet with the teacher-coordinator to get her assessment of the program's needs, talk with the principal, and, if need be, go to the school board. When they met with the teacher, she told them about the challenges she faced—a schedule that barely allowed her enough time to drive between schools, lack of materials to use with the kids, little planning time during the day, the unconcerned attitude about gifted education among administrators. She felt unappreciated and isolated because no one in the district seemed to consider her work a serious priority.

Then the parents decided to meet with the principal. They made specific suggestions, which they had discussed with the teacher:

1. Hire a consultant from a nearby university to hold a series of workshops to help classroom teachers meet the needs of their gifted students (thus taking some of the burden off the gifted teacher).

2. Provide time for the gifted teacher to assist other teachers in their efforts to modify the curriculum for gifted students.

3. Solicit parent volunteers to help with students' activities and projects.

4. Investigate additional funding sources, such as local companies that give money to schools for specific projects.

The principal suggested they meet with the superintendent. When they called the superintendent, she asked them to submit their concerns and proposals to her in writing. They did so, and requested a meeting to discuss the feasibility of their suggestions. At the meeting, the superintendent endorsed their ideas, with a few minor adjustments. She then advised them on how to make a presentation to the school board. She also gave them the name of a board member with a gifted child in the district, suggesting that they approach him before addressing the board. This board member proved instrumental in promoting their cause at board meetings. When the group finally did present their ideas to the school board, many members were receptive.

Gradually, the board made gifted education a greater priority. Once they did, change began to happen. The school arranged for a student teacher specializing in gifted education at the local university to help the gifted teacher both with teaching and coordinating. The next year, funding was provided for a series of workshops for teachers on differentiating instruction to challenge their gifted students. The pull-out program continued, but with increased funding for resources. The teacher-coordinator was allowed time both for planning and for assisting classroom teachers. Parents helped by working with students and finding resources for independent student projects.

The group of four parents expanded to twelve. They formed an organization, appointed officers, drew up bylaws, and began to meet regularly. They also became a resource for other parents interested in starting a group.

Take a Stand!

Think about specific ways you could support your child and yourself by connecting with other parents of gifted kids. Do you want to help your child form new friendships with other high-ability kids? Would you like to learn how other parents deal with social and emotional issues at home and at school? Are you interested in sharing ideas for creating or expanding gifted education programs in your child's school or district? Decide on something specific you'd like to gain or accomplish by getting to know and work with another parent or other parents. Then take the first step to make a parent-to-parent connection.

Chapter 11

Advocacy Is . . .
Taking a Stand in Gifted Education

Our district's philosophy statement on gifted education recognizes children with academic, creative, and artistic talent. But in my son's school, kids aren't eligible for the gifted program unless they score at least 130 on the group intelligence test given in the spring. They also need to be recommended by their classroom teacher.

My son Gabriel is creatively gifted, and his talents don't show up well on tests. When he was in third grade, his teacher told me that the quality of Gabe's work sometimes startled him. He noticed Gabe's exceptional drawing ability, the unusually perceptive comments he often made about what he'd read, and original approaches he'd suggest to solving math problems. At the same time, the teacher noted, my son's work was messy, and he was absent-minded, often late with his assignments. I asked the teacher if he'd recommend Gabe for the gifted program, but he said between the average test scores and the "issues with self-discipline and organization," Gabe just didn't qualify.

That year I showed the gifted education coordinator some of Gabe's work and quoted the teacher's comments about his exceptional abilities. But the coordinator said that it wouldn't be fair to let Gabe in the program, that all children should have the same requirements. I've gradually learned that our district pays only lip service to the idea of including creatively gifted students. I don't think anyone there really understands how differently these kids approach learning. The coordinator herself told me the school's G/T program probably wouldn't work for him even if he could get in. Apparently, students are free to take unique approaches to their work, but there's no specific attempt to encourage thinking "outside the box," and the program is rigidly run and heavily academic. She actually told me that my best bet would be to find Gabe an art class somewhere, buy him math puzzles, and subscribe to a science magazine!

Well, Gabe got through third grade somehow. I tried to provide opportunities for him myself. We'd take some of his assignments and do side projects. Once he created a short story out of a math problem he had to do. He and I weathered the complaints from the teacher about his inattentiveness and sloppy homework as best we could.

In fourth grade, Gabe's teacher understood that his inattentiveness and procrastination were due to boredom. She arranged for Gabe to work independently in the art room whenever he finished his classwork on time. She also allowed him to skip certain assigned work if he could show he'd mastered it, and she gave him projects that allowed him to use his offbeat approach to solving problems. At the end of the year, I asked her to write her own evaluation of Gabe and what she thought he needed. She was sympathetic about my frustrations and wrote a glowing report with many specific descriptions of his abilities and potential.

Now he's in fifth grade, and it's the same old story. The teacher reports that Gabe won't pay attention, does sloppy work, and turns it in late. This year, I went to the principal with the fourth-grade teacher's detailed report of Gabe's gifts. I also brought in examples of Gabe's work and talked to the principal about my son's preferred intelligences. To my surprise, he was sympathetic. But when I mentioned the district's philosophy statement and said I felt the school wasn't responding to creatively gifted kids, he stiffened. He said he hoped to improve the gifted program, but funding is limited and it will take time. He advised me to be patient.

Patient? I've been working on this for three years. If I'm any more patient, my son will graduate before the school does anything to meet his learning needs. Two of Gabe's friends are a lot like him, and I've been talking to their parents about taking the issue up with the school board.

Gabriel's parent saw a clear gap between policy (gifted services are to include creatively talented students) and practice (only students with high test scores and teacher recommendations are admitted). When a school is unwilling to take seriously this kind of discrepancy, parents need to consider an organized effort for change.

Advocating for changes in policy or practice has its own unique challenges. Working with other parents is essential in this situation, because it is a collective effort that's most likely to impel decision makers to listen.

You'll want to consider forums other than the school if:

- the school seems unable or unwilling to help you in your advocacy

- school staff members are sympathetic, but lack funding or authorization to make changes

- you see a discrepancy between policy and practice

- you see the need to influence policy

Gabriel's mother needs first to organize and amplify her notes on all her solo efforts to improve her son's education. She needs details: dates, records of conferences and other communication efforts, her own observations of her son and their conversations about his school experiences.

Next, she needs to continue working with fellow parents who have similar concerns. Even one or two other parents can amplify her call for change. These parents should pool their notes and create a report that presents the traits their kids have, what these characteristics mean for the kids' learning needs, how the school is falling short, and what the parents would like the school to do to change the situation.

The next step will most likely be to meet with the district superintendent to apprise him or her of their position and initiate a dialogue. It's best to meet with the superintendent as a group, share the written record, and clearly outline their concerns, experiences, and suggestions. Most superintendents understand that parents are a powerful constituency and that even a small group of concerned parents should be listened to. Also, the superintendent usually has some power to make changes in how the gifted program is administered.

In your own group's efforts to enforce or alter policy, a great deal may depend on the relationship between the school board and the superintendent. School boards hire superintendents, and superintendents may function differently depending on the governing style of the board. Some school boards micromanage districts far more than others, and this affects the kind of decision-making power the superintendent has. However, most superintendents have the authority to act on such issues as unfair identification procedures or discrepancies between district policy on gifted education and actual practices in the schools.

TAKE YOUR CASE TO THE SCHOOL BOARD

After meeting with the superintendent, the next step is to go to the school board. School boards make decisions about curriculum, staff, and expenditures. The school board and superintendent decide whether to institute and maintain a gifted program. They also select identification criteria, determine the age or grade when students will begin gifted programming, and decide what form the program will take (pull-out classes, magnet schools, or differentiated curriculum, for example). Perhaps most important, it's often the superintendent and the board who together decide whether to allocate money for gifted education from general district funds *in addition* to state funds specifically earmarked for gifted programming.

Do Your Homework

Before you can make a presentation requesting policy changes, you have to do the research that will lay the groundwork:

Know your state laws. Familiarize yourself with what (if anything) is required by your state's laws governing gifted education.

Learn how your district is funded. Understanding how your district acquires funding will assist you in your efforts to create more opportunity for gifted students. Funding that supplements programs for students with special needs is often called *categorical funds.* These funds are designated for specific groups of students, such as those who qualify for gifted programs based on the state's definition of giftedness.

How districts translate the state's definition into their own requirements for acceptance into a program varies. But every district must use its categorical funds for the student population it has defined and for the programs it has described in its application to the state. Find out (from your state association, gifted education coordinator, or principal) what your school's individual allocation is and how the school is supposed to use the funds.

Check out what other districts are doing. Find out about the gifted program in one or two other, similar-sized districts. Compare these approaches with your district's program.

Know what others in your district want. Consider doing an informal needs assessment survey of parents and teachers to see what interested people think should be changed. In the process, you may find other parents—and perhaps teachers—who might be willing to assist you in your presentation to the board. One or two supportive teachers can go a long way to help advance your cause. With their involvement, you'll be able to show the board that both parents and teachers are concerned about the learning needs of gifted students.

Know the schedule. Early in your advocacy, familiarize yourself with the board's yearly schedule—particularly, when decisions are made concerning funding for gifted education. Find out when the board schedules presentations (often early in the school year).

Learn about the styles and views of school board members. Elected by the community, members devote many hours to a daunting task with no pay and often with little recognition. Most school board members are involved because of their genuine interest and concern, but they also may have their own agendas for education (for example, a member may want to change the math curriculum in the district). This is why it is important to become aware of who the board members are and what positions they hold on various issues. Do some research on your district's board by consulting with a parent group, talking to teachers, and attending school board meetings. Board meetings are also often broadcast on public-access TV. This can offer a helpful introduction, but attending in person will help you become a recognized presence and give you a first-hand sense of the board's dynamics.

Get a feel for how topics are discussed and how individual members tend to respond to specific issues. You need to know which members are sympathetic to your concerns, and which aren't. Observing carefully for a few meetings will tell you a lot about how individual members are likely to respond to a request for improvements in gifted education.

Know what the board is presently working on. School board members often have to make difficult decisions. Your advocacy at this level needs to be well planned and coordinated in order to have a strong impact. Before making a presentation, be aware of the kinds of issues the board is currently dealing with. This tells you something about the board's priorities and workload, and may help you time your presentation or relate it to current issues of concern to the board.

With the background information and understanding of the school board in place, ask the superintendent or a board member to request a time for your group to make a presentation to the board on what's needed for the gifted program.

Make Your Presentation

You'll want to plan your presentation well. If you can win supporters on the board, there's a good chance for changes at school. Here are some key points to consider in preparing and presenting your case:

- **Clarify the broad issue.** A school board is less likely to institute changes for one child than for a population of students. Think about your issue as it affects all gifted kids or a particular group of gifted kids. Is there an identification problem? A curriculum problem? A funding problem?

- **Use facts to substantiate your position.** Be prepared to provide pertinent data. It always helps to have an understanding of the significance of your concern in terms of the population of students affected. For example, if you'd like to see broader criteria used for admission to the gifted program, you may want to investigate how a narrow identification method eliminates various potentially gifted students—for example, children from diverse cultures, children with learning differences or disabilities, or creatively gifted children. Use the Internet or check with your state gifted association to get some data from studies done by educational researchers. Such data will show the board that you're requesting something that has been identified as a critical issue by professionals in the field.

Why Should Districts Support Gifted Education?

NAGC has solid background information that can help you state your case and offers these reasons for supporting gifted education:*

- Gifted learners must be given stimulating educational experiences appropriate to their level of ability if they are to realize their potential.

- Each person has the right to learn and to be provided challenges for learning at the most appropriate level where growth proceeds most effectively.

- At present, only slightly over one-half of the possible gifted learners in the United States are reported to be receiving education appropriate to their needs.

- Traditional education currently does not sufficiently value bright minds.

- When given the opportunity, gifted students can use their vast amount of knowledge to serve as a background for unlimited learning.

- Providing for our finest minds allows both individual and societal needs to be met.

---

* National Association for Gifted Children Web site, April 2001. Go to *www.nagc.org/ParentInfo/index.html* for an expanded explanation.

- **Be organized.** Prepare your notes or statement so your message is clear and easy to follow. Get right to the point. First state the purpose of your visit, explaining your concern and what you'd like to see changed. Next, describe the sequence of your own advocacy at your child's school. Make it clear that you've come to the board because you've exhausted all other avenues.

- **Educate.** If your school has no services for gifted students, explain clearly why services are needed. Talk about gifted students as an underserved minority—a group with special needs that aren't being met. Make a strong case for the fact that gifted children often do not thrive without support—that many tend to under-achieve, withdraw, or develop behavior problems. Support your argument with examples and statistics. Emphasize that helping gifted kids thrive is crucial to the future of all of us. School board members are usually not educators. They may know little or nothing about gifted children or gifted education. It's up to you to inform them.

- **Show the evidence.** If you'd like improvement in existing programs and services, be prepared to explain the ways the current opportunities fall short for your child and others. Have examples available to demonstrate your point. Present any evidence or research that supports your position, such as statements from other parents, the results of a survey your parent group conducted, or studies on the issue by experts in gifted education.

- **Provide handouts.** Have a succinct handout to give board members that highlights your concerns, the evidence that backs them up, and the steps you'd like to see instituted to make a change.

- **Be flexible.** You want to state your views and present your case clearly and forcefully—but you don't want to offend or alienate board members. Suggest both long-term and short-term goals, and recommend flexible timelines for meeting them. Know what you want, and don't let yourself be distracted by emotional reactions, your own or other people's. Focus on the policies that need changing. Be hard on the problem but patient with the people— including yourself. If you find that you're dealing with bureaucrats, remember that a bureaucracy is based on rules and regulations. Present different ways to think about problems.

- **Summarize.** Summarize your issue and what you're requesting. Thank board members for the opportunity to address them.

Don't give up on board members if at first they seem resistant. Be patient with your efforts, and with theirs. Even if the board supports your concerns and proposals, changes in district policy take time. Throughout the process, try to stay in touch with a board member who seems interested or sympathetic. This person can keep you informed of any developments, request additional information from you, and advise you about follow-up steps to take.

Our son Joe was bored and unchallenged in school, and we hadn't gotten much help from the school staff. At a neighborhood gathering, we happened to meet a member of the school board. We explained our dilemma and found her very interested in our concerns. She urged us to make a presentation to the board and helped us prepare and arrange it. As she recommended, we incorporated some research we'd done on gifted students into our presentation, and several board members seemed impressed. Soon after, they initiated a serious inquiry into the school's gifted population, looking at what was being done to accommodate the educational needs of these students. The first thing that happened was that the district applied for funding from the state. The district also created a gifted education coordinator position, part time at first, full time within the next two years. Even before this coordinator began, the superintendent scheduled a series of workshops for regular classroom teachers on meeting the needs of their gifted students.

By the time the coordinator started, she found several teachers who had already begun to modify their curriculum. Our son's teacher was one of them. She allowed Joe to test out of material he already knew, do independent projects, and read more advanced books. And now that the district has funding for gifted education, Joe is eligible for other opportunities, like a pull-out program twice a week.

Like these parents, your purpose is to build bridges. See the board members as potential advocates for your gifted child and others. Invite their questions and encourage further interaction.

TAKE YOUR CASE TO THE STATE

Since opportunities for your child largely depend on the funds your school and district acquire from the state, you may want to consider taking your advocacy to the state level.

Doing this is not as daunting as it may sound. You can begin by getting to know your elected legislators. Find out when legislative sessions adjourn; most legislators spend at least some time in their home offices when the legislative body is not in session, and this may be a good time to meet your local representative. Find out when your legislator will be in and call or write a letter requesting a meeting. Mention what you want to discuss.

To prepare for this meeting, consult your state gifted association. There is no doubt that legislators respond more readily to organized groups who represent a large membership than to individuals. Becoming a member of a state gifted advocacy organization can save you a lot of time. Most organizations have an intimate knowledge of the legislative process. They are actively engaged in advocacy at the state level and understand the position various legislators have on gifted education. By contacting them, you can coordinate your individual efforts with their campaigns. You'll also learn about the steps involved in the passage of a bill and how funds that support existing programs are allocated each year.

How Can You Make the Most of a Meeting with a Legislator?

Here are some useful steps to consider when planning to meet with your state legislator:

1. Call or write a letter requesting a meeting with your elected decision-maker stating the topic for discussion and asking when he or she would be available. If other advocates plan to attend with you, include their names. If there is no response within a reasonable time, place a follow-up call.

2. Prepare in advance so you can clearly make your points in less than half an hour. Review information supporting your request for action.

3. At the meeting, introduce yourself and other advocates with you. (Three to four advocates should be an easily accommodated number for an office conference.)

4. Tell your legislator why you are there.

5. If possible, leave printed information for later review.

6. Always write a thank-you note expressing appreciation for your elected decision-maker's time and for his or her consideration of your request. Also, include any information the person requested.

* *Advocacy in Action: An Advocacy Handbook for Gifted and Talented Education* (California Association for the Gifted, page 33).

Don't be discouraged if you end up meeting with an aide. Legislators' aides often play a major role in the development of legislation. After the meeting, stay in touch with your legislator as much as possible. Attend functions where your representative is to make a scheduled appearance; reintroduce yourself at these events. Request that you be on the person's mailing list for anything pertaining to education issues.

Find out when it's best to write letters or make phone calls in support of or against specific bills under consideration. Timing is very important, because you want to contact legislators when any bill concerning gifted education comes up for a vote. State gifted-education advocacy organizations often publish newsletters to inform parents of issues that need addressing, bills up for discussion, what potential laws and regulations will mean for gifted children, and when committee and full-body hearings and votes will take place. Your state organization may also provide letter templates for specific issues, ideas about how to write your own letters and what information to include, as well as effective scripts for phone calls and face-to-face meetings.

Sometimes, advocacy organizations may encourage parents to present testimony at special hearings that affect the future of gifted education in the state. Parent testimony can be powerful. State legislators want to know how the programs they fund are working or why changes or additional money allocations are needed—your personal experiences can make a strong and lasting impact.

If you do have the opportunity to speak at a hearing, speak about the state's gifted children, not just those in your school or district. Do be prepared to provide examples of how children's needs are going unmet and/or how, specifically, the legislation being considered will affect gifted children in the state. Again, your state gifted organization can provide ongoing research information and data to support your position or proposal.

State Government: Find Out More

If your state gifted organization doesn't offer resources regarding state policy-level advocacy, here are two useful books you'll find at your library reference desk and one organization to look into:

State Code. Every state publishes its own code book, which lists laws that pertain to that state. The *State Code* is usually updated every legislative session.

State Legislative Leadership, Committees, and Staff (The Council of Governments, printed annually). This volume will tell you which of your legislators serve on which committees.

National Conference of State Legislatures (NCSL)
444 North Capitol Street NW, Suite 515
Washington, DC 20001
(202) 624-5400
www.ncsl.org
The NCSL tracks what's happening state-by-state on a variety of issues including education.

Take a Stand!

Attend a school board meeting. Go to the meeting with another parent of a gifted child. Bring your notebook to keep track of your observations. Note any board members who seem open to parents' concerns and to the needs of children from diverse backgrounds. Even if gifted services aren't under discussion, a member who seems objective and broadly interested in the needs of all children, including those from diverse backgrounds, may be open to questions and concerns about gifted education. Notice also which board members seem well spoken, passionate about particular issues, or well informed.

You may not feel ready to lobby your school board on behalf of gifted children. However, you'll be in a much more knowledgeable position to advocate at any level if you get acquainted with your school board, how it works, what issues it's currently considering, and what interests and biases its members seem to have.

Chapter 12
Advocacy Is . . . Taking Care of Yourself

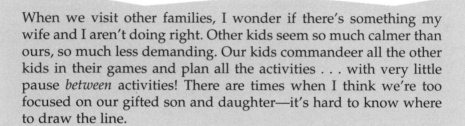

When we visit other families, I wonder if there's something my wife and I aren't doing right. Other kids seem so much calmer than ours, so much less demanding. Our kids commandeer all the other kids in their games and plan all the activities . . . with very little pause *between* activities! There are times when I think we're too focused on our gifted son and daughter—it's hard to know where to draw the line.

Sometimes I wish I had an average kid. My daughter never stops, never takes a break—never gives *me* a break!

Many parents of gifted children feel like satellites around a great ball of energy! It's easy to feel overwhelmed by the responsibilities of parenthood, particularly when you're the parent of a gifted young person—your child brings so much more to the process than you anticipated! And it's difficult to remember you have a life of your own when your child pulls you in so many directions at once.

HOW MUCH IS TOO MUCH?

As the parent of a gifted child, you're probably pretty focused on your child's unique abilities, talents, learning styles, and needs. As your child's advocate, you want to stay informed and current about his school experiences. When parents get involved in helping their child, they often begin to remember some of their own school experiences, both good and bad. Possibly without realizing it, you may be identifying on a personal level with difficulties your child is facing in school or in relationships with other kids. Such identification can make your desire to help all-consuming, your focus almost entirely on your child. The result of this might be that you become *too* involved.

At six, Vanessa was already reading at a fifth-grade level. All through first and second grade, I was embroiled in discussions with teachers, the gifted education coordinator, and the principal to help Vanessa get what she needed from school. It wasn't easy. I could see eyes roll when I walked into the principal's office. I'm sure I was a regular pain. The more I struggled, the more intense and hyper I became about my daughter's education. My husband and I also began to argue. He would say, "Look at her! She's doing all right. We'll work this out." But I couldn't hear him. Thinking back, I see that I was over the top, treating my daughter like she was in the emergency room or something.

What changed this for me was meeting other parents in a group I found out about. One of the topics under discussion was how easy it is to become completely wrapped up in your kids' lives, to the point where you're living through them. We talked about how unhealthy that is for everyone involved. One parent made a remark that really struck me. "You know," she said, "we forget how resilient our kids are. Sure they need our help and support, but they're not as fragile as we sometimes think."

Since that meeting, I've tried to give myself some fresh air—reconnecting with old friends, taking a workshop or class at the nearby college, exercising, reading, and just slowing down a little. I've consciously tried to be less emotionally invested in Vanessa's needs. I think people at school are listening to me more since I've stopped acting like a firefighter trying to rescue my daughter from a burning building.

It's important to remind yourself that your child is neither weak nor helpless. His sensitivity can make him vulnerable to difficult situations, but he's also capable of becoming stronger and more flexible as he goes along. Yes, it's your job to be there for your child. It's also your job to give him room to develop on his own. A gifted child who's constantly shielded and protected may never gain the skills he needs to cope with challenging circumstances.

Gifted kids need to know that the world won't come to an end if they're having a problem in school. One of the ways they learn this is by observing how their parents respond when a problem surfaces. Kids don't want to see us bent out of shape on their behalf. Imagine how you would feel if you were a child and your parents were excessively worried about your well-being. You'd hear them making tense phone calls to school personnel, see them hovering in the halls to talk with your teachers, and feel their anxiety and frustration. It's a burden for children to witness their parents stressed in this way—and on their behalf. Some react by becoming less communicative—they won't tell their parents about their troubles in school so Mom or Dad won't have to struggle on their behalf.

Are You Out of Balance?

How do you know when you're being over-involved with your child? Ask yourself these questions:

- Do I spend most of the day thinking and worrying about my gifted child?

- Do I contact the teacher over every little issue that comes up?

- Do I see my child as a fragile being who could easily be damaged by school?

- Do I expect the whole family to accommodate our gifted child's special needs? Do I sacrifice family gatherings and time for other family members so that this child doesn't miss any opportunities?

- Have I created such a full schedule for my child that he has little time to relax, read, spend time with friends, or just be a kid?

- Are concerns about my child my chief topic of conversation?

- Do I push my child to do things even if I suspect he's not interested?

- Do I get upset if my child doesn't make the high grades I know he's capable of?

- If my child has problems in school, do I feel this is a reflection of my parenting?

If you answer yes to some or all of these questions, you run the risk of living *through* your child, of allowing his challenges and achievements to become the central focus of your life. This is unhealthy for both of you.

What you most need in your relationship with your gifted child is balance. You are important to your child, and your child is important to you—but you are both individuals. Balance comes through stepping back, freeing yourself from vicarious identification with everything your child experiences and does. Realize that your job isn't to come between your child and his experience, but to support his ability to learn, grow, and thrive in different environments. Remind yourself that having a gifted child is a challenging adventure, not a burden, and that you are a coach and mentor, not a martyr.

GIVE YOURSELF SOME FRESH AIR

One of the most difficult parts of advocacy is keeping *yourself* going—not letting criticism deflate you, not letting closed doors defeat you, not letting emotions distract you from your goal—and, simultaneously, not neglecting to sustain your own life, too. You need support and people to talk to. You need feedback and a sense of perspective.

Whatever your circumstances, give yourself some "fresh air." Time and space for yourself are essential. No matter how difficult it may seem to manage, try and carve out some little niche in the day or week to do something you love. Rediscover a hobby or an interest—watch birds, play racquetball, walk or run, do yoga, read mysteries. Don't let yourself become so depleted by the demands of your gifted child that you feel empty and drained. Give of your light, but not of your oil.

It's easy to become so immersed in helping our kids that we forget they're watching us to see how they should feel about learning, how they should respond to challenges, how they should act when things don't go their way, how they should value their own personal interests and needs. E. Paul Torrance, the great pioneer in creativity research, had a marvelous piece of advice for gifted kids in an article he wrote for *Creative Child and Adult Quarterly*. You may find, as I do, that it applies just as well to parents of gifted kids:*

1. Don't be afraid to fall in love with something and pursue it with intensity and depth.

2. Know, understand, take pride in, practice, develop, use, exploit, and enjoy your greatest strengths.

3. Learn to free yourself from the expectations of others and to walk away from the games that others try to impose upon you. Free yourself to "play your own game" in such a way as to make good use of your gifts.

4. Don't waste a lot of expensive energy trying to do things for which you have little ability or love. Do what you can do well and what you love, giving freely of the infinity of your greatest strengths and most intense loves.

---

* "The Importance of Falling in Love with Something" by E. Paul Torrance, in *Creative Child and Adult Quarterly* 8, no. 2 (1983), page 78.

You may not realize how much your child benefits from seeing you involved in things, interested in the world around you, enjoying life. Nothing is so energizing to a gifted child as a parent showing great interest in some activity or pursuit—from martial arts to gardening to politics to basketball. A wonderful reciprocity can develop in families where parents and children share in each other's interests. Children grow up with living examples of what it means to love learning and to pursue one's passions with energy and determination.

Instead of "hovering over your child's shoulder," let her hover over yours. Let her see what you enjoy doing, what you love learning. Think about how you can involve your child in activities that interest you. For example, if you like to write, consider creating stories together. One parent I know, an environmentalist, taught her children how to test water samples near their home.

Take a Stand!

Think about yourself as a person in your own right. What are your needs? What would you like to do if you had the time? What would you like to *make* time for? Maybe you'd like to do carpentry work, refinish furniture, draw, sew, take workshops in art or photography, catch up with friends, join a book club, keep a journal, play volleyball, take up music lessons you started as a child, dream about new possibilities, or think more deeply about life. How can you set aside time to do this? Can you find a little time for yourself each day? Every other day? Twice a week? Once a week?

Start however you can. Start big or start small. But make the start. As you replenish yourself, you'll be renewing your energy and zest for all of the many other facets of the life and support you share with your partner, your family, your work, your friends—and your gifted child.

A FINAL WORD

We do a great service to our gifted children when we help them find a sense of purpose—by our own personal example and by guiding them and giving them room to grow. Many gifted young people get good grades and plenty of praise, but this does not always satisfy them. They're hungry for something more individually fulfilling. They long to feel connected to humanity and the universe in a deep, meaningful way.

When we as parents help our gifted children discover their niche in the world, we're helping them claim a reason for being. This is the essence of what we work for in our advocacy. The author bell hooks pays tribute to this kind of advocacy when she tells of the extraordinary women in her family who helped her to stand on her own feet. Speaking of the influence her grandmother's quiltmaking had on her, she writes:

> Fascinated by the work of her hands, I wanted to know more, and she was eager to teach and instruct, to show me how one comes to know beauty and give oneself over to it. To her, quiltmaking was a spiritual process where one learned surrender. . . . This was the way she had learned to approach quilt- making from her mother. To her it was an art of stillness and concentration, a work which renewed the spirit.*

Hooks goes on to explain how she found inspiration for her own work from the quilt her grandmother gave her:

> Since my creative work is writing, I proudly point to ink stains on this quilt which mark my struggle to emerge as a disciplined writer. . . . This quilt (which I intend to hold onto for the rest of my life) reminds me of who I am and where I have come from.**

The quilt performed a special service for bell hooks. It affirmed in a tangible way her heritage, a heritage she could look at and remember whenever she needed to. Woven into the fabric of the quilt was also the strength, sureness, and deep spirituality of her grandmother, who gave bell hooks the special support she needed to embrace her own gifts.

It's my fervent desire that this book fulfill a similar purpose for you and, through you, for your child. I've tried to show how you as a parent can make and share your own quilt, invested with passion, commitment, affirmation,

---

* *Yearning: Race, Gender, and Cultural Politics* by bell hooks (Boston: South End Press, 1990), page 116.
** hooks, pages 121–122.

and the courage to create. Work steadily but patiently on your quilt. Take fulfillment in both its beauty and its flaws. Involve your child in the process so your gifted daughter or son can claim and continue the process of expanding the quilt and creating new designs and beauty.

You can give your child no greater gift.

GLOSSARY OF TERMS

ability grouping
Putting together students (either on a temporary or permanent basis) with similar skills for instruction in a particular subject area such as math or reading.

achievement tests
Tests that measure what students have learned or have been taught, measured against the expected achievement of average students.

ADHD (attention deficit hyperactivity disorder)
A condition with symptoms that include problems with being overly physically active and having difficulty sitting still or paying attention. ADHD should be diagnosed by a doctor. It's not unusual for teachers to think a child has ADHD when in fact the real problem is a lack of stimulation in the classroom.

asynchronous development
Development in which intellectual growth is ahead of physical and emotional development.

categorical funds
Funding that supplements programs for students with special needs. Categorical funds are designated for specific groups of students, such as those who qualify for gifted programs based on the state's definition of giftedness.

ceiling of difficulty
A top level of performance that a test can assess.

cluster grouping
Grouping students of the same grade level who have been identified as gifted in the same class and heterogeneously mixing the other students.

cooperative learning
An instructional method in which students work cooperatively in similar or mixed-ability groups.

curriculum compacting

An instructional method in which material is compressed into a shortened time frame and a student is allowed to demonstrate mastery of content already known, often through pretests.

differentiation

A process of adapting the regular classroom curriculum to meet each student's individual learning needs.

ESL

An abbreviation used in schools to mean English as a second language. ESL students are those who are learning English and whose first language is not English.

flexible grouping

Varying the way students are grouped for instruction and learning based on interests and abilities on an assignment-by-assignment basis.

gifted

Having advanced intellectual ability, a high degree of creativity, or heightened sensibilities with outstanding capability or potential for performing at remarkably high levels of accomplishment when compared with others of similar age, experience, or environment.

G/T

An abbreviation used in some schools, meaning gifted and talented.

heterogeneous grouping

Grouping students of all levels and abilities together.

homeschooling

Being taught full or part time at home rather than in a public or private school, usually by a parent or another relative.

identification

Methods used to recommend students for gifted services.

intelligence tests

Tests, like the Stanford-Binet, that measure children's potential to do well in intellectual pursuits.

IQ (intelligence quotient)
A measure of how well a child can complete intellectual tasks that compares the child's mental age to the child's actual age. A high IQ score represents potential and does not reflect creativity or motivation to achieve.

LD
An abbreviation used in schools to mean learning differences. LD refers to neurological impairment that interferes with the brain's ability to process information. For example, dyslexia is a form of LD that causes some people to perceive letters and words incorrectly.

learning contract
An agreement made between a teacher and a student that includes a description of a project or activity a child will do, what the child is expected to accomplish, goals to meet along the way, a timeline, and rules of behavior.

LEP
An abbreviation used in schools to mean limited English proficiency. LEP students are those who are learning English and whose first language is not English.

mastery learning
A teaching method in which students advance through the curriculum according to ability rather than grade level; this option allows students to move through material at their own pace.

mentorship
A learning relationship with an adult (a mentor) who specializes in a particular subject, discipline, or career. The mentor helps guide and develop the student's skills and interests.

multiple criteria
Several methods schools use to identify gifted children, such as creativity tests, parent input, and portfolio reviews.

multiple intelligences
Different ways of taking in information and thinking about it. Identified by Harvard psychologist Howard Gardner, the eight intelligences are linguistic, musical, logical-mathematical, visual-spatial, bodily-kinesthetic, interpersonal, intrapersonal, and naturalistic. Each individual has relative strengths and weaknesses among these intelligences.

norm-referenced tests

Tests developed and carefully monitored for validity with students of a particular grade, age, region of the country, gender, or other characteristics. A child's score reflects how he/she compares to other students like him/her in various ways at the national, state, or local level. Also called standardized tests.

standardized tests

Tests developed and carefully monitored for validity with students of a particular grade, age, region of the country, gender, or other characteristics. A child's score reflects how she/he compares to other students like her/him in various ways at the national, state, or local level. Also called norm-referenced tests.

tiered assignments

Placing students together, usually based on ability or learning style, to work on a particular topic or project, enabling the teacher to target the learning needs of each group of students in relation to a specific assignment. Tiered assignments allow the teacher to assign gifted students an especially challenging topic. This practice avoids permanent grouping arrangements; students change groups as their abilities improve.

tracking

Grouping students permanently by ability. A typical example of tracking is placing students in "low," "middle," and "advanced" reading groups.

twice exceptional

Both gifted and having a physical, an emotional, or a learning disability.

underachievement

A student's abilities significantly exceed performance. An underachieving student is not necessarily a gifted child, but underachievement has become a major concern among advocates for the gifted.

BIBLIOGRAPHY

Adderholdt, Miriam and Jan Goldberg. *Perfectionism: What's Bad about Being Too Good?* Revised and updated edition. Minneapolis: Free Spirit Publishing, 1999.

Alvino, James. *Parents' Guide to Raising a Gifted Child: Recognizing and Developing Your Child's Potential from Preschool to Adolescence.* New York: Ballantine Books, 1996.

American Association of University Women (AAUW). *How Schools Shortchange Girls.* Washington, DC: American Association of University Women Educational Foundation, 1992.

Baum, Susan M., Steven V. Owen, and John Dixon. *To Be Gifted and Learning Disabled: From Identification to Practical Intervention Strategies.* Mansfield Center, CT: Creative Learning Press, 1991.

Benson, Peter L., Judy Galbraith, and Pamela Espeland. *What Kids Need to Succeed: Proven, Practical Ways to Raise Good Kids.* Revised, expanded, updated edition. Minneapolis: Free Spirit Publishing, 1998.

Bireley, Marlene. *Crossover Children: A Sourcebook for Helping Children Who Are Gifted and Learning Disabled.* Second edition. Arlington, VA: The Council for Exceptional Children, 1995.

California Association for the Gifted (CAG). *Advocacy in Action: An Advocacy Handbook for Gifted and Talented Education,* 1998.

California Association for the Gifted (CAG). *Advocating for Gifted English Language Learners: An Activity Handbook for Professional Development and Self-Study,* 1999.

California Association for the Gifted (CAG). *The Challenge of Raising Your Gifted Child,* 1998.

California Association for the Gifted (CAG). *Joining Forces: A Guide to Forming Support Organizations for Gifted and Talented Children,* 1998.

Clark, Barbara. *Growing Up Gifted: Developing the Potential of Children at Home and at School.* Fifth edition. Upper Saddle River, NJ: Prentice Hall, 1997.

Clark, Rosemarie, Donna Hawkins, and Beth Vachon. *The School-Savvy Parent: 365 Insider Tips to Help You Help Your Child.* Minneapolis: Free Spirit Publishing, 1999.

Cline, Starr. *Giftedness Has Many Faces: Multiple Talents and Abilities in the Classroom.* Delray Beach, FL: Winslow Press, 2000.

Cohen, LeoNora and Erica Frydenberg. *Coping for Capable Kids: Strategies for Students, Parents, and Teachers.* Waco, TX: Prufrock Press, 1996.

Davis, Gary A. and Sylvia B. Rimm. *Education of the Gifted and Talented.* Fourth edition. Needham Heights, MA: Allyn & Bacon, 1997.

Delisle, Deb and James Delisle. *Growing Good Kids: 28 Activities to Enhance Self-Awareness, Compassion, and Leadership.* Minneapolis: Free Spirit Publishing, 1997.

Delisle, Jim and Judy Galbraith. *When Gifted Kids Don't Have All the Answers: How to Meet Their Social and Emotional Needs.* Minneapolis: Free Spirit Publishing, 2001.

Esquivel, Giselle and John C. Houtz, eds. *Creativity and Giftedness in Culturally Diverse Students.* Cresskill, NJ: Hampton Press, 2000.

Flack, Jerry. D. *TalentEd: Strategies for Developing the Talent in Every Learner.* Englewood, CO: Teacher Ideas Press, 1993.

Ford, Donna Y. *Reversing Underachievement Among Gifted Black Students: Promising Practices and Programs.* New York: Teachers College Press, 1996.

Frasier, Mary M. and A. Harry Passow. *Toward a New Paradigm for Identifying Talent Potential.* Storrs, CT: National Research Center on the Gifted and Talented, 1994.

Galbraith, Judy. *The Gifted Kids' Survival Guide: For Ages 10 and Under.* Revised edition. Minneapolis: Free Spirit Publishing, 1999.

Galbraith, Judy. *You Know Your Child Is Gifted When . . . A Beginner's Guide to Life on the Bright Side.* Minneapolis: Free Spirit Publishing, 2000.

Gallagher, James J. and Shelagh A. Gallagher. *Teaching the Gifted Child.* Fourth edition. Needham Heights, MA: Allyn & Bacon, 1994.

Gardner, Howard. *Intelligence Reframed: Multiple Intelligences for the 21st Century.* New York: Basic Books, 1999.

Gellman, Estelle S. *School Testing: What Parents and Educators Need to Know.* Westport, CT: Greenwood Publishing Group, 1995.

Goleman, Daniel. *Emotional Intelligence: Why It Can Matter More Than IQ.* New York: Bantam Books, 1997.

Gross, Miraca U.M. *Exceptionally Gifted Children.* London: Routledge, 1993.

Jones, Claudia. *More Parents Are Teachers, Too: Encouraging Your 6- to 12-Year-Old.* Charlotte, VT: Williamson Publishing Co., 1990.

Karnes, Francis A. and Ronald G. Marquardt. *Gifted Children and Legal Issues: An Update.* Scottsdale, AZ: Gifted Psychology Press, 2000.

Karnes, Francis A. and Suzanne M. Bean. *Girls and Young Women Inventing: Twenty True Stories About Inventors Plus How You Can Be One Yourself.* Minneapolis: Free Spirit Publishing, 1995.

Katz, Elinor. *Affective Education: Self Concept and the Gifted Student.* Boulder, CO: Open Space Communications, 1994.

Kay, Kiesa., ed. *Uniquely Gifted: Identifying and Meeting the Needs of the Twice Exceptional Student.* Gilsum, NH: Avocus Publishing, 2000.

Kerr, Barbara A. *Smart Girls: A New Psychology of Girls, Women, and Giftedness.* Scottsdale, AZ: Gifted Psychology Press, 1997.

Kingore, Bertie. *Portfolios: Enriching and Assessing All Students: Identifying the Gifted Grades K–6.* Des Moines, IA: Leadership Publishers, 1993.

Knopper, Dorothy. *Parent Education: Parents as Partners.* Boulder, CO: Open Space Communications, 1997. (Also available in Spanish.)

Kurcinka, Mary Sheedy. *Raising Your Spirited Child: A Guide for Parents Whose Child Is More Intense, Sensitive, Perceptive, Persistent, Energetic.* New York: HarperCollins, 1992.

Lazear, David. *Pathways of Learning: Teaching Students and Parents about Multiple Intelligences.* Tucson, AZ: Zephyr Press, 2001.

Meador, Karen S. *Creative Thinking and Problem Solving for Young Learners.* Englewood, CO: Libraries Unlimited, 1998.

Milgram, Roberta M., ed. *Counseling Gifted and Talented Children: A Guide for Teachers, Counselors, and Parents.* Stamford, CT: Ablex Publishing, 1991.

Olenchak, F. Richard. *They Say My Kid's Gifted: Now What?* Waco, TX: Prufrock Press, 1998.

Perry, Susan K. *Playing Smart: The Family Guide to Enriching, Offbeat Learning Activities for Ages 4–14.* Minneapolis: Free Spirit Publishing, 2001.

Piirto, Jane. *Talented Children and Adults: Their Development and Education.* Second edition. Upper Saddle River, NJ: Prentice Hall, 1998.

Piirto, Jane. *Understanding Those Who Create.* Scottsdale, AZ: Gifted Psychology Press, 1998.

Porter, Louise. *Gifted Young Children: A Guide for Teachers and Parents.* St. Leonards NSW, Australia: Allen and Unwin, 1999.

Ray, Brian D. *Strengths of Their Own: Home Schoolers Across America: Academic Achievement, Family Characteristics, and Longitudinal Traits.* Salem, OR: National Home Education Research Institute, 1997.

Reis, Sally. *Work Left Undone: Choices and Compromises of Talented Women.* Mansfield Center, CT: Creative Learning Press, 1998.

Reis, Sally, D. E. Burns, and Joseph Renzulli. *Curriculum Compacting: The Complete Guide to Modifying the Regular Curriculum for High Ability Students.* Mansfield Center, CT: Creative Learning Press, 1992.

Renzulli, Joseph S. and Linda H. Smith. *The Learning Styles Inventory.* Mansfield Center, CT: Creative Learning Press, 1978.

Rimm, Sylvia. *Dr. Sylvia Rimm's Smart Partenting: How to Parent So Children Will Learn.* New York: Crown Publishing, 1997.

Rimm, Sylvia. *Keys to Parenting the Gifted Child.* Hauppauge, NY: Barron's Educational Series, 2001.

Rivero, Lisa. *Gifted Education Comes Home: A Case for Self-Directed Homeschooling.* Manassas, VA: Gifted Education Press, 2000.

Roeper Review, "The Young Gifted Child." Vol. 21, no. 3, 1999.

Rupp, Rebecca. *The Complete Home Learning Source Book.* New York: Three Rivers Press, 1998.

Saunders, Jacqulyn with Pamela Espeland. *Bringing Out the Best: A Guide for Parents of Young Gifted Children.* Minneapolis: Free Spirit Publishing, 1991.

Sisk, Dorothy. *Creative Teaching of the Gifted.* New York: McGraw-Hill, 1987.

Smutny, Joan Franklin, ed. *Underserved Gifted Populations.* Cresskill, NJ: Hampton Press, 2001.

Smutny, Joan Franklin, ed. *The Young Gifted Child: Potential and Promise, an Anthology.* Cresskill, NJ: Hampton Press, 1998.

Smutny, Joan Franklin, Kathleen Veenker, and Stephen Veenker. *Your Gifted Child: How to Recognize and Develop the Special Talents in Your Child From Birth to Age Seven.* New York: Ballantine Books, 1991.

Smutny, Joan Franklin, Sally Yahnke Walker, and Elizabeth A. Meckstroth. *Teaching Young Gifted Children in the Regular Classroom: Identifying, Nurturing, and Challenging Ages 4–9.* Minneapolis: Free Spirit Publishing, 1997.

Tomlinson, Carol Ann. *How to Differentiate Instruction in Mixed-Ability Classrooms.* Second edition. Alexandria, VA: Association for Supervision and Curriculum Development, 1998.

Torrance, E. Paul. *Discovery and Nurturance of Giftedness in the Culturally Different.* Reston, VA: Council for Exceptional Children. 1977.

Torrance, E. Paul and Dorothy Sisk. *Gifted and Talented Children in the Regular Classroom.* Buffalo, NY: Creative Education Foundation, 1998.

Torrance, E. Paul, Kathy Goff, and Neil B. Satterfield. *Multicultural Mentoring of the Gifted and Talented.* Waco, TX: Prufrock Press, 1997.

Walker, Sally Yahnke. *The Survival Guide for Parents of Gifted Kids: How to Understand, Live With, and Stick Up for Your Gifted Child.* Minneapolis: Free Spirit Publishing, 1991.

Webb, James T. and Arlene R. DeVries. *Gifted Parent Groups: The SENG Model.* Scottsdale, AZ: Gifted Psychology Press Inc., 1998.

Webb, James T., Elizabeth A. Meckstroth, and Stephanie S. Tolan. *Guiding the Gifted Child: A Practical Source for Parents and Teachers.* Scottsdale, AZ: Gifted Psychology Press, 1989.

Winebrenner, Susan. *Teaching Gifted Kids in the Regular Classroom.* Revised, expanded, updated edition. Minneapolis: Free Spirit Publishing, 2001.

OTHER RESOURCES

ORGANIZATIONS

California Association for the Gifted
5777 West Century Boulevard,
Suite 1670
Los Angeles, CA 90045
(310) 215-1898
www.cagifted.org

The Center for Gifted
National-Louis University
2840 Sheridan Road
Evanston, IL 60201
(847) 256-5150, ext. 2150
www.centerforgifted.com

Council for Exceptional Children (CEC)
1110 North Glebe Road, Suite 300
Arlington, VA 22201-5704
1-888-232-7733
www.cec.sped.org/index.html

Educational Assessment Service, Inc.
W6050 Apple Road
Watertown, WI 53098
1-800-795-7466
www.sylviarimm.com

Education Program for Gifted Youth (EPGY)
Ventura Hall
Stanford University
Stanford, CA 94305-4115
1-800-372-3749
www-epgy.stanford.edu

ERIC Clearinghouse on Disabilities and Gifted Education
1110 North Glebe Road
Arlington, VA 22201-5704
1-800-328-0272
ericec.org

The Gifted Child Society
190 Rock Road
Glen Rock, NJ 07452-1736
(201) 444-6530
www.gifted.org

Gifted Development Center
1452 Marion Street
Denver, CO 80218
(303) 837-8378
www.gifteddevelopment.com

Hollingworth Center for Highly Gifted Children
827 Center Avenue, #282
Dover, NH 03820-2506
www.hollingworth.org

Home School Legal Defense Association (HSLDA)
P.O. Box 3000
Purcellville, VA 20134
(540) 338-5600
www.hslda.org

Illinois Association for Gifted Children (IAGC)

800 East Northwest Highway
Suite 610
Palatine, IL 60067-6512
(847) 963-1892
www.iagcgifted.org

National Association for Gifted Children (NAGC)

1707 L Street NW, Suite 550
Washington, DC 20036
(202) 785-4268
www.nagc.org

The National Foundation for Gifted and Creative Children

395 Diamond Hill Road
Warwick, RI 02886
(401) 738-0937
www.nfgcc.org/index.html

National Home Education Research Institute (NHERI)

P.O. Box 13939
Salem, OR 97309
(503) 364-1490
www.nheri.org

National Research Center on the Gifted and Talented (NRC/GT)

University of Connecticut
2131 Hillside Road, Unit 3007
Storrs, CT 06269
(860) 486-4676
www.gifted.uconn.edu/nrcgt.html

National Women's History Project

7738 Bell Road
Windsor, CA 95492-8518
1-800-691-8888
www.nwhp.org

Parents of Gifted and Talented Learning-Disabled Children

2420 Eccleston Street
Silver Spring, MD 2090
(301) 986-1422

Texas Association for the Gifted and Talented

406 East Eleventh Street, Suite 310
Austin, TX 78701-2617
(512) 499-8248
www.txgifted.org

Torrance Center for Creative Studies

Department of Educational Psychology
The University of Georgia
Athens, GA 30602-7146
(706) 542-5104
www.coe.uga.edu/torrance

PUBLISHERS AND PUBLICATIONS

A.W. Peller
210 Sixth Avenue
P.O. Box 106
Hawthorne, NJ 07507
1-800-451-7450
www.awpeller.com
A distributor for more than 100 publishers, producers, and manufacturers
of educational materials, its *Bright Ideas for the Gifted and Talented* catalog features products such as books, kits, videos, posters, games, and CD-ROMS
for gifted students K–12.

Cobblestone Publishing Company
30 Grove Street, Suite C
Peterborough, NH 03458
1-800-821-0115
www.cobblestonepub.com
Cobblestone is a publisher of high-quality nonfiction magazines for young
readers such as *Click, Ladybug,* and *Ask* for grades preK–4, and *Cricket,
Footsteps,* and *Calliope* for grades 4 and up. It uses the expertise of editors, writers, and advisors in a variety of fields to produce magazines on history, world
cultures, science, and other subjects in an interesting and engaging way.

Creative Learning Press
P.O. Box 320
Mansfield Center, CT 06250
1-888-518-8004
www.creativelearningpress.com
Creative Learning Press provides a variety of manuals and activity books
for teachers working with gifted children including, Renzulli and Reis's
best-selling *Schoolwide Enrichment Model* and Reis's *Work Left Undone:
Choices and Compromises of Talented Females.* It offers an extraordinary
Mentors-in-Print section with a wide range of stimulating, hands-on, how-
to books for gifted children at all grade levels.

Critical Thinking Books and Software
P.O. Box 448
Pacific Grove, CA 93950
1-800-458-4849
www.criticalthinking.com
Producer of one of the largest selections of high quality critical thinking
products for K–adult education, its products aim to improve academic performance, encourage students of all ability levels, and extend achievement
for future success.

Dandy Lion Publications

3563 Sueldo, Suite L
San Luis Obispo, CA 93401
1-800-776-8032
www.dandylionbooks.com
Dandy Lion is a leading publisher of educational teaching materials that stress development of creative and critical thinking for students in grades K–8. It presents innovative methods for teaching all subjects, and is ideal for teachers in gifted and talented programs, teachers in regular classrooms, homeschoolers, and parents.

Free Spirit Publishing

217 Fifth Avenue North, Suite 200
Minneapolis, MN 55401-1299
1-800-735-7323
www.freespirit.com
An award-winning publisher of nonfiction resources for children and teens, parents, educators, and counselors, Free Spirit develops a variety of research-based and user-friendly materials on such topics as self-esteem and self-awareness, stress management, school success, creativity, friends and family, peacemaking, social action, and special needs (i.e., gifted and talented, learning differences).

Gifted Education Communicator (formerly known as *Communicator*), featuring articles by national leaders in the field, parent-to-parent articles, and hands-on curriculum. See the entry for California Association for the Gifted (page 175) for more information.

Gifted Education Press

10201 Yuma Court
P.O. Box 1586
Manassas, VA 20108
(703) 369-5017
www.cais.com/gep
Gifted Education Press is a publisher of books and periodicals on educating gifted children offering a wide range of innovative materials for teachers, parents, homeschoolers, and students on all subjects for all grade levels and distributes materials in school districts across the nation.

Gifted Psychology Press
P.O. Box 5057
Scottsdale, AZ 85261
(602) 954-4200
www.giftedpsychologypress.com
Gifted Psychology Press is a publisher of books for parents, teachers, counselors, and educators of gifted and talented children that focus on subjects such as guiding gifted students, creativity, college planning, self-esteem, legal issues, girls, mentorship, parent advice, and more.

The Journal is a yearly journal that features articles on specific topics such as underserved populations, young gifted children, and teaching strategies for gifted students in the regular classroom. See the entry for the Illinois Association for Gifted Children (page 176) for more information.

New Moon Publishing
P.O. Box 3620
Duluth, MN 55803
1-800-381-4743
www.newmoon.org
New Moon is the publisher of *New Moon: The Magazine for Girls and Their Dreams, New Moon Network: For Adults Who Care About Girls,* books for girls, and curricula and learning activities for all grades that correspond with each issue of *New Moon.* New Moon is an invaluable resource for teachers, homeschoolers, and girls' group leaders.

Open Space Communications, Inc.
1900 Folsom, Suite 108
Boulder, CO 80302
1-800-494-6178
www.openspacecomm.com
A Colorado-based company that serves those who live and work with gifted children, Open Space produces books and tapes and also publishes *Understanding Our Gifted,* a journal for teachers and parents. Several resources are also available in Spanish.

Parenting for High Potential is a quarterly magazine for parents published by the National Association for Gifted Children. It includes suggestions for activities to do with your child as well as the latest Web sites, technology, and educational toys, all reviewed by experts in the field. See page 176 for more information.

Phi Delta Kappa International
408 North Union Street
P.O. Box 789
Bloomington, IN 47402-0789
1 800-766-1156
www.pdkintl.org
Phi Delta Kappa is a publisher of books for grades K–12, including "fastback" booklets. Topics include gifted girls and an overview of gifted education. They also publish *Phi Delta Kappan,* a professional print journal for education.

Pieces of Learning
Division of Creative Learning Consultants Inc.
1990 Market Road
Marion, IL 62959
1-800-729-5137
www.piecesoflearning.com
Pieces of Learning is a publisher and producer of K–12 supplementary enrichment activity books, resource books, and parenting and staff development videos. Topic areas include critical and creative thinking, questioning skills, and materials for subjects such as language arts, math, writing, literature, thematic learning, research, and much more.

Prufrock Press
P.O. Box 8813
Waco, TX 76714-8813
1-800-998-2208
www.prufrock.com
Prufrock is a publisher of innovative products and materials that support the education of gifted and talented children and also provides teachers and parents of gifted children a comprehensive online education resource, a listing of gifted children links and products, gifted education magazines (e.g., *Gifted Child Today*), research journals, identification instruments, books, and more.

Roeper Review
P.O. Box 329
Bloomfield Hills, MI 48303
www.roeperreview.org
This journal covers a broad range of issues for professionals who work with teachers and psychologists, and for professionals who work directly with gifted and talented children and their families. The journal provides coverage of policy issues, developments, innovations in practice, and applied research. It emphasizes both the cognitive and the emotional.

Skipping Stones: A Multicultural Magazine

P.O. Box 3939
Eugene, OR 97403
(541) 342-4956
www.treelink.com/skipping/main.htm
Skipping Stones is a nonprofit children's magazine that encourages cooperation, creativity, and celebration of cultural and environmental richness. It provides a forum for sharing ideas and experiences among children from different lands and backgrounds.

TEMPO is a journal published four times a year by the Texas Association for the Gifted and Talented. The journal focuses on gifted education and features articles on a variety of themes such as leadership, identification, and homeschooling (see page 176).

Thinking Caps

P.O. Box 26239
Phoenix, AZ 85068
(602) 870-1527
Publisher of educational materials for the gifted. Although primarily designed for teachers, parents can use this source to supplement their children's education. Materials based on Bloom's taxonomy.

Thinking Works

P.O. Box 468
St. Augustine, FL 32085
1-800-633-3742
Distributor of educational materials from a variety of publishers. Extensive selection useful to both teachers and parents.

Tin Man Press

P.O. Box 11409
Eugene, OR 97440
1-800-676-0459
www.tinmanpress.com
Tin Man publishes original thinking-skills materials for the elementary grades that are applicable for a broad range of enrichment applications and in gifted programs.

Zephyr Press
3316 North Chapel Avenue
Tucson, AZ 85716
(520) 322-5090
zephyrpress.com
Zephyr is a publisher of educational materials that focuses on the multiple intelligences theory. The activities within the products integrate disciplines so that learning is more meaningful. Products are designed for educators or parents, and tools are practical, easy to use, and incorporate the latest research.

WEB SITES ON GIFTED

A Glossary of Gifted Education
members.aol.com/svennord/ed/GiftedGlossary.htm

GT World! A Meeting Place for Families and Friends of the Gifted and Talented
www.gtworld.org

Hoagies' Gifted Education Page
www.hoagiesgifted.org

Surfing the Net with Kids
www.surfnetkids.com

TAG Family Network
www.teleport.com/~rkaltwas/tag

TAG Project
www.tagfam.org

Talent Development Resources
TalentDevelop.com

Welcome to the Gifted Resources Home Page
www.eskimo.com/~user/kids.html

Whole Family Center
www.wholefamily.com

WEB SITES ON HOMESCHOOLING

Families Learning About Giftedness (FLAG)
members.aol.com/LrningAtHm/flagindex.html

Homeschooling Resources for Gifted Students
www.cec.sped.org/ericec/minibibs/eb18.htm

Learn in Freedom!
learninfreedom.org

INDEX

ABOUT THE AUTHOR

Founder of The Center for Gifted at National-Louis University, Joan Franklin Smutny directs programs for thousands of gifted children and young people. She teaches creative writing to children in her programs and courses on gifted education for graduate students. Her extensive works in the field are often published and/or cited in professional literature, and she presents at local and national seminars, on television, and on radio. She is cochair of Membership as well as Special Schools and Programs Division for the National Association for Gifted Children. She is also editor of the *IAGC Journal* and contributing editor for *Understanding Our Gifted, Roeper Review: A Journal on Gifted Education,* and for *Gifted Education Press Quarterly.* Joan coauthored *Your Gifted Child: How to Recognize and Develop the Special Talents in Your Child from Birth to Age Seven* (with Kathleen Veenker and Stephen Veenker: Ballantine Books, 1989), *A Thoughtful Overview of Gifted Education* (with Judy W. Eby: Longman, 1990), and *Teaching Young Gifted Children in the Regular Classroom* (with Sally Walker and Elizabeth Meckstroth: Free Spirit Publishing, 1997). In 1998, she wrote *Gifted Girls,* a "fastback" booklet for Phi Delta Kappa and anticipates the publication of *Gifted Education: Promising Practices for the 21st Century* (Phi Delta Kappa, 2002). In addition, Joan is responsible for two edited volumes, *The Young Gifted Child: Potential and Promise, an Anthology* (Hampton Press, 1997) and *Underserved Gifted Populations* (Hampton Press, 2001). In 1996, she received the NAGC Distinguished Service Award for outstanding contribution to the field of gifted education.

Other Great Books from Free Spirit

You Know Your Child Is Gifted When...
by Judy Galbraith, M.A., illustrated by Ken Vinton, M.A.
This one-of-a-kind book makes it fun and easy to learn the basics about what makes gifted kids "tick" and how you can support their unique abilities. A light-hearted introduction to life with a young gifted child, it blends humorous cartoons and lively illustrations with solid information on giftedness—its characteristics, challenges, and joys. For parents and educators of gifted children in grades PreK–6. *$10.95; 128 pp.; softcover; illus.; 6" x 6"*

Teaching Young Gifted Children in the Regular Classroom
Identifying, Nurturing, and Challenging Ages 4–9
by Joan Franklin Smutny, M.A., Sally Yahnke Walker, Ph.D., and Elizabeth A. Meckstroth, M.Ed., M.S.W.
Written for educators (and parents) who believe that all children deserve the best education we can give them, this guide encourages and enables you to identify gifted children as early as age 4 and create a learning environment that supports all students. For preschool through grade 4. *$29.95; 240 pp.; softcover; 8½" x 11"*

The Gifted Kids' Survival Guide
For Ages 10 & Under
Revised & Updated Edition
by Judy Galbraith, M.A.
First published in 1984, newly revised and updated, this book has helped countless young gifted children realize they're not alone, they're not "weird," and being smart, talented, and creative is a bonus, not a burden. Includes advice from hundreds of gifted kids. For ages 10 & under. *$9.95; 104 pp.; softcover; illus.; 6" x 9"*

The Gifted Kids' Survival Guide
A Teen Handbook
Revised, Expanded, and Updated Edition
by Judy Galbraith, M.A., and Jim Delisle, Ph.D.
Vital information on giftedness, IQ, school success, college planning, stress, perfectionism, and much more. For ages 11–18.
$14.95; 304 pp.; softcover; illus.; 7¼" x 9¼"

When Gifted Kids Don't Have All the Answers
How to Meet Their Social and Emotional Needs
by Jim Delisle, Ph.D., and Judy Galbraith, M.A.
Gifted kids are much more than test scores and grades. Topics include self-image and self-esteem, perfectionism, multipotential, depression, feelings of "differentness," and stress. Includes first-person stories, easy-to-use strategies, survey results, activities, reproducibles, and up-to-date research and resources.
$17.95, softcover, 192 pp., illust., 7¼" x 9¼"

Playing Smart
The Family Guide to Enriching, Offbeat Learning Activities for Ages 4–14
Revised, Expanded, & Updated Edition
by Susan K. Perry, Ph.D.
Our new edition of a family favorite offers hundreds of fun, educational ways to promote creative thinking, laughter, learning, and loving relationships. From making walks interesting to creating a family book of world records, these simple, satisfying activities rely on little more than family commitment. Includes recommended resources and Web sites that point the way toward more adventures. *$16.95; 240 pp.; softcover; illus.; 7¼" x 9¼"*

The Survival Guide for Parents of Gifted Kids
How to Understand, Live With, and Stick Up for Your Gifted Child
by Sally Yahnke Walker
Up-to-date information about giftedness, gifted education, problems, personality traits, and more, written by an educator of gifted kids and their parents. For parents of children ages 5 & up. *$10.95; 152 pp.; softcover; illus.; 6" x 9"*

Bringing Out the Best
A Guide for Parents of Young Gifted Children
Revised and Updated
by Jacqulyn Saunders with Pamela Espeland
This popular handbook explains how to tell if your child is gifted, how to choose the right school, how to deal with teachers, and more. Includes activities to do together and tips for avoiding parent burnout. For parents of children ages 2–7.
$14.95; 240 pp.; softcover; B&W photos and illus., 7¼" x 9¼"

The School-Savvy Parent
365 Insider Tips to Help You Help Your Child
by Rosemarie Clark, M.Ed., Donna Hawkins, M.Ed., and Beth Vachon, M.Ed.
Who knows the most about how to prepare your child for a happy, safe, successful school year? Teachers! Straight from the source, here are hundreds of positive, practical tips all parents can use to become active, informed supporters of their children's education. For parents of children ages 4–14. *$12.95; 208 pp.; softcover; illus.; 5" x 8"*

What Kids Need to Succeed
Proven, Practical Ways to Raise Good Kids
Revised, Expanded, and Updated Edition
by Peter L. Benson, Ph.D., Judy Galbraith, M.A., and Pamela Espeland
Our new edition of a proven best-seller identifies 40 developmental "assets" kids need to lead healthy, productive, positive lives, then gives them more than 900 suggestions for building their own assets at home, at school, in the community, and in the congregation. Parents' Choice approved. For parents, teachers, community and youth leaders, and teens. *$5.99; 256 pp.; softcover; 4⅛" x 6⅛"*

What Young Children Need to Succeed
Working Together to Build Assets from Birth to Age 11
by Jolene L. Roehlkepartain and Nancy Leffert, Ph.D.
Based on groundbreaking research, this book helps adults create a firm foundation for children from day one. You'll find hundreds of practical, concrete ways to build 40 assets in four different age groups. Comprehensive, friendly, and easy-to-use, this book will make anyone an asset builder and a positive influence in children's lives. For parents, teachers, all other caring adults, and children. *$9.95; 320 pp.; softcover; illus.; 5¼" x 8"*

What Teens Need to Succeed
Proven, Practical Ways to Shape Your Own Future
by Peter L. Benson, Ph.D., Judy Galbraith, M.A., and Pamela Espeland
Based on a national survey, this book describes 40 developmental "assets" all teens need to succeed in life, then gives hundreds of suggestions teens can use to build assets at home, at school, in the community, in the congregation, with friends, and with youth organizations. For ages 11 & up. *$14.95; 368 pp.; softcover; illus.; 7¼" x 9¼"*

To place an order or to request a free catalog of SELF–HELP FOR KIDS® and SELF–HELP FOR TEENS® materials, please write, call, email, or visit our Web site:

Free Spirit Publishing Inc.
217 Fifth Avenue North • Suite 200 • Minneapolis, MN 55401-1299
toll-free 800.735.7323 • local 612.338.2068 • fax 612.337.5050
help4kids@freespirit.com • www.freespirit.com

Visit us on the Web!

www.freespirit.com

Stop by anytime to find our Parents' Choice Approved catalog with fast, easy, secure 24-hour online ordering; "Ask Our Authors," where visitors ask questions—and authors give answers—on topics important to children, teens, parents, teachers, and others who care about kids; links to other Web sites we know and recommend; fun stuff for everyone, including quick tips and strategies from our books; and much more! Plus our site is completely searchable so you can find what you need in a hurry. Stop in and let us know what you think!

Just point and click!

new! Get the first look at our books, catch the latest news from Free Spirit, and check out our site's newest features.

contact Do you have a question for us or for one of our authors? Send us an email. Whenever possible, you'll receive a response within 48 hours.

order! Order in confidence! Our secure server uses the most sophisticated online ordering technology available. And ordering online is just one of the ways to purchase our books: you can also order by phone, fax, or regular mail. No matter which method you choose, excellent service is our goal.

1.800.735.7323 • fax 612.337.5050 • help4kids@freespirit.com